Editor
Mara Ellen Guckian

Editor in Chief
Brent L. Fox, M. Ed.

Creative Director
Sarah M. Fournier

Cover Artist
Sarah Kim

Illustrator
Mark Mason

Art Coordinator
Renée Mc Elwee

Imaging
Amanda R. Harter

Publisher
Mary D. Smith, M.S. Ed.

For standards correlations, visit *http://www.teachercreated.com /standards/*.

LET'S GET THIS 2
DAY STARTED
Science

TCR 8262

- Start the day off right with engaging, standards-based science passages and writing activities.

- Each unit includes non-fiction passages, vocabulary activities, and supplemental worksheets. All content is designed to encourage students to "show what they know."

- Unit activities help students improve comprehension skills from recall to critical thinking.

- Photographs or illustrations are provided to boost student understanding of important science concepts.

Teacher Created Resources

Author
Tracy Edmunds, M.A. Ed.

Teacher Created Resources
12621 Western Avenue
Garden Grove, CA 92841
www.teachercreated.com
ISBN: 978-1-4206-8262-5

© 2020 Teacher Created Resources
Made in U.S.A.

Table of Contents

Introduction 4

How to Use This Book 5

Life Science

Unit 1: Living Things
Traits of Living Things 6
What Is a Plant? 7
What Is an Animal? 8
Plant or Animal? 9
Living or Nonliving? 10

Unit 2: All About Plants
Parts of Plants 11
Parts of Plants We Eat 12
Plants Need Sunlight 13
Plants Need Water 14
Plants in Different Places 15

Unit 3: Plant Reproduction
Plant Life Cycles 16
Pollination 17
Seed Dispersal: Wind and Water 18
Seed Dispersal: Animals 19
Seed Dispersal: People 20

Unit 4: Fun with Plants
Plant Defenses 21
Plants That Eat Meat 22
Record-Breaking Plants 23
The School Garden 24
Design a Plant 25

Unit 5: Animal Needs
What Animals Need 26
Animals Need Oxygen 27
Animals Need Water 28
Animals Need Food 29
Animals Need Shelter 30

Unit 6: Animal Habitats
What Is a Habitat? 31
Living and Nonliving Parts of Habitats 32
Omnivores Have Options 33
Wet or Dry? 34
Migration 35

Unit 7: Vertebrate Animals
Mammals 36
Birds 37
Reptiles 38
Amphibians 39
Fish 40

Unit 8: Invertebrate Animals
Insects 41
Insect Body Parts 42
Arachnids 43
Crustaceans 44
Gastropods 45

Earth and Space Science

Unit 9: Seasons
What Are Seasons? 46
Summer 47
Fall 48
Winter 49
Spring 50

Unit 10: Weather
What Is Weather? 51
Weather Reports 52
Reading a Weather Report 53
Dangerous Weather 54
Rainbows 55

Table of Contents *(cont.)*

Unit 11: Earth Changes

Slow Changes to Earth: Part 1 56
Slow Changes to Earth: Part 2 57
Volcanoes 58
Earthquakes 59
Water Changes the Land 60
Quick or Slow Change? 61

Unit 12: Water on Earth

The Water Cycle 62
Where Is the Water on Earth? 63
Salt Water 64
Ice on Earth 65
Keep Water Clean 66

Unit 13: Landforms

Landforms 67
Mountains and Hills 68
Valleys and Canyons 69
Plains 70
People Change the Land 71

Unit 14: Bodies of Water

Water on Earth 72
Oceans 73
Rivers and Streams 74
Lakes 75
People Change Water on Earth 76

Unit 15: Maps

What Is a Map? 77
Map Keys and Symbols 78
Compass Rose 79
What Is a Globe? 80
Comparing Maps and Globes 81

Physical Science

Unit 16: Properties of Materials

What Are Properties of Materials? 82
Describing Properties of Materials 83
Observing with the Senses 84
Uses of Materials 85
Changing Properties of Materials 86

Unit 17: States of Matter

Matter 87
Solids 88
Liquids 89
Gases 90
Changing States of Matter 91

Unit 18: Reversible and Irreversible Changes

Two Kinds of Changes 92
Freezing and Melting 93
Changes That Can't Be Reversed 94
Can It Change Back? 95

Unit 19: Heat, Light, and Sound Energy

Heat, Light, and Sound Energy 96
Heat 97
Light 98
Sound 99
What Kind of Energy? 100

Science and Engineering Practices

Unit 20: About Science

What Do Scientists Do? 101
Data Measurement 102
Interpreting Data 103
Scientists Look for Patterns 104
Cause and Effect 105

Tracking Sheet 106

Answer Key 107

Introduction

Science is the study of the world around us. Students experience science every day without knowing it! Learning about how the world works can be fascinating, but sometimes, students must find fun and accessible science topics *before* they realize how enjoyable science can be. The passages in this book contain high-interest topics that will immediately hook students and allow them to see science at work in their own experiences. From how hummingbirds help flowers make seeds to finding out how much of Earth's fresh water is frozen, students will enjoy practicing their informational reading skills with interesting science topics.

This book is arranged into four sections:

Life Science

Physical Science

Earth and Space Science

Science and Engineering Practices

Within each section are a number of units, each of which explores an important science topic. Most pages feature reading passages and response questions. Some pages include science-related worksheets. Within each science discipline, the units are sequential and build upon one another, and pages are sequential within a unit.

Teachers should not feel restricted by a daily warm-up activity. Sometimes, schedules change. A morning assembly, a make-up lesson, or just an extra-busy day can easily throw off the classroom schedule for days. A teacher never knows what his or her week is going to look like. *Let's Get This Day Started: Science* units do not need to be completed every day or even every other day. Teachers can take their time and arrange the activities to fit their own schedules. A teacher may choose to do a unit a week (one passage a day), or, at other times, spread a unit out over a few weeks. There is no right or wrong way.

These pages are meant to be a supplement, not a substitute, for a science curriculum. Use them in conjunction with science lessons whenever possible.

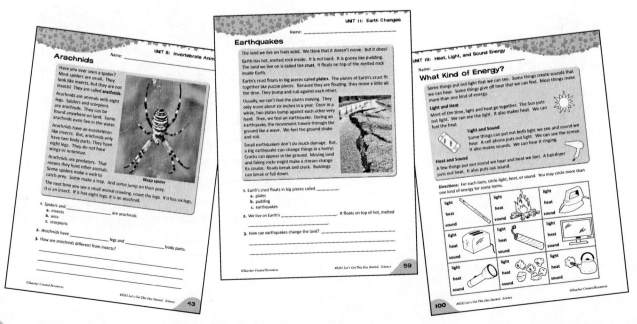

How to Use This Book

When introducing each new science topic, a teacher may choose to have the class read the passages together as a group before asking them to read each passage again on their own. A teacher may also choose to have students reread passages after a science lesson or unit to reinforce and review learning.

Note: Some units incorporate photographs in student activities. These add a realistic element to the writing prompts and engage students by providing a real-life connection for their learning. When making photocopies of these pages, it is best to use the photo setting so the images are easier to see. You may also choose to supplement certain passages with related photographs or other visual aids you might have available.

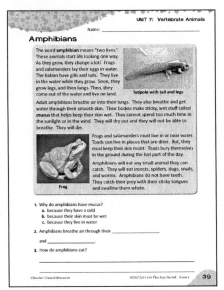

The multiple-choice questions in *Let's Get This Day Started: Science* assess all levels of comprehension—from recall to critical thinking. These questions offer an opportunity to teach students test-taking skills. If an answer choice includes an unfamiliar word, the correct answer can still be found by the process of elimination. Remind students to read every answer choice! If the answer doesn't jump out at them, they can get it right by crossing out the wrong answers first.

The missing words or phrases for fill-in-the-blank questions can be found within the reading passage. These questions reinforce important scientific vocabulary and concepts.

Short, written-response questions require students to connect new learning to their own experience or to apply the concepts in the passage to a new situation. These questions are intended to encourage students to "show what they know," and responses will vary based on students' reading, writing, and prior knowledge.

Use the *Tracking Sheet* on page 106 to keep track of which passages you have given to your students, or distribute copies of the sheet for students to monitor their own progress.

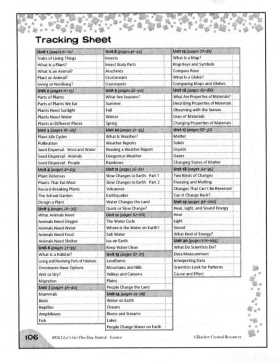

Name: _____

Traits of Living Things

Plants and animals are living things. How do we know something is living?

○ Living things use energy to move and grow.
Plants get their energy from the Sun.
Animals get their energy from the food they eat.

○ Living things need water.
Plants get water through their roots.
Most animals drink water.

○ Living things need air.
Plants take in air through their leaves.
Animals breathe air into their lungs or gills.

○ Living things grow and change.
Both plants and animals get bigger.
They change as they grow.

○ Living things make more of themselves.
Plants make seeds. Seeds grow new plants.
Animals have babies. The babies grow
into adults.

1. Living things use _____ to move and grow.
   a. seeds
   b. energy
   c. lungs

2. Living things make more of _____.

3. Name two ways you know something is living.

   Something is living if _____

   _____

   _____

Name: _____

What Is a Plant?

There are many kinds of plants. Some plants you may know are trees and grasses. You can eat some plants. When you eat an apple or lettuce, you are eating a plant.

Plants make their own food. They need sunlight, air, and water. They turn these things into energy. They use the energy to move and grow.

Plants can move. They move so slowly that you might not see them move. Plants can turn toward the Sun. Flowers can open and close.

Plants make more of themselves. Most plants have flowers. Flowers make seeds. Seeds can grow new plants. A tomato seed grows a tomato plant. A pine tree seed grows a pine tree.

Some kinds of plants can make copies of themselves without seeds. Potato plants grow out of potatoes.

1. Plants make their own _____.
    a. sunlight
    b. water
    c. food

2. What kind of plant will grow from a sunflower seed? _____

3. Can plants move?   **Yes**   **No**

How do they move? _____

_____

_____

Name: _____

What Is an Animal?

There are many kinds of animals. Some are very big, like elephants. Some are very small. They are so small that you might not see them.

All animals need food. They turn food into energy to move and grow. Some animals eat plants. Cows and snails eat plants. Some animals eat meat. That means that they eat other animals. Lions and sharks eat other animals. Some animals eat both plants and meat. Bears and chickens eat some plants and some meat.

All animals need air. Animals that live on land breathe air into their lungs. Most animals that live under water breathe through their gills.

All animals **reproduce**. This means that they make animals like themselves.

Some animals have babies. A gorilla has a baby. The baby grows up to be an adult gorilla.

Some animals lay eggs. Robin eggs hatch into baby robins. They grow up to be adult robins.

Frog eggs hatch into tadpoles. Tadpoles change as they grow and turn into frogs.

1. Animals turn the food they eat into _____.
   a. energy   **b.** meat   **c.** plants

2. What does *reproduce* mean?
   a. turn food into energy   **b.** make more of themselves   **c.** breathe air in

3. Write three facts that are true about all animals.

   Fact 1: _____

   _____

   Fact 2: _____

   _____

   Fact 3: _____

   _____

Name: _____

Plant or Animal?

Scientists put things in groups. This makes it easier to study them. The two main groups for living things are **plants** and **animals**.

Directions: Be a scientist and help sort the living things. Write the name of each living thing in the animal or plant group.

Cheetah

Baobab tree

Hummingbird

Snail

Raspberry bush

Barrel cactus

Snake

Dandelion

Animals

_____

_____

_____

_____

_____

Plants

_____

_____

_____

_____

_____

Name: _____

Living or Nonliving?

Directions: Read the questions. Write *Yes* or *No* in the chart to answer each one.

Living or Nonliving	Dog 	Chair 	Rock 	Tree 
Does it use energy?				
Does it need water?				
Does it need air?				
Does it grow and change?				
Does it make more of itself?				
Is it living?				

Name: _____

Parts of Plants

Plants have parts that help them grow and survive:

➡ Plants drink in water through their **roots**. They also get nutrients from the soil.

➡ The **stem** carries the water up into the plant.

➡ **Leaves** use water, air, and sunlight to make food for the plant.

➡ **Flowers** make seeds that will grow new plants.

➡ **Fruits** protect seeds and help them find new places to grow.

1. Label each plant part. Use the **boldface** words above.

a. _____   b. _____

c. _____

d. _____

e. _____

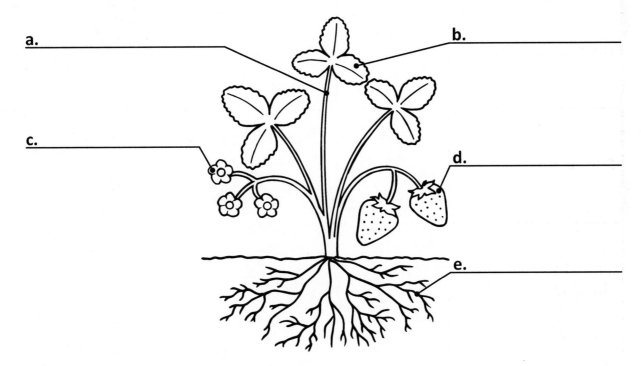

2. Which part of the plant makes food?

   a. roots   **b.** stem   **c.** leaves

3. Plants drink in water through their _____.

4. What do flowers do to help plants? _____

_____

_____

Name: _____

Parts of Plants We Eat

Do you eat plants? What parts of plants do you eat?

➡ Have you eaten broccoli or cauliflower? You were eating flowers!

➡ When you eat lettuce, spinach, or cabbage, you are eating leaves.

➡ We eat the fruits of many different plants. Tomatoes, peppers, pumpkins, apples, oranges—so many fruits!

➡ When you eat celery or asparagus, you are eating a stem.

 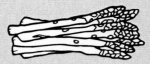

➡ When you eat an onion, a carrot, or a radish, you are eating roots.

➡ We eat the seeds of sunflowers, corn, and pea plants.

Directions: For each food, write which part of the plant we eat. You will only use each word from the Word Bank once.

Word Bank	flower	fruit	leaf	root	seed	stem

1. carrot _____

2. broccoli _____

3. spinach _____

4. apple _____

5. corn _____

6. asparagus _____

Name: _____

Plants Need Sunlight

How do you get your energy? You eat food. Do plants eat food? No, they do not. So, how do plants get energy? They make it!

Plants have leaves. There is a special green **chemical** in the leaves. That is why leaves are green! This green chemical uses sunlight to make food for the plant. The food gives the plant energy to grow.

Plants need sunlight to make food. They need water, air, and nutrients, too.

Have you ever played with building blocks? You can rearrange them. That means that you can take them apart and put them together a different way. You can make different things with them.

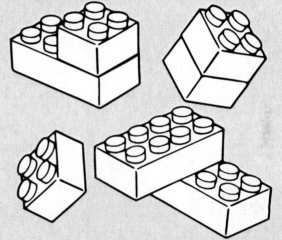

Molecules are like very tiny building blocks. Everything is made of molecules. Sunlight helps plants take apart water and air molecules. The smaller parts get rearranged into food for the plant.

1. Plants need water, sunlight, and air to make _____.
    a. leaves
    b. chemicals
    c. food

2. Sunlight helps plants take apart _____ and

    _____ molecules.

3. How do plants make their own food? _____

    _____

    _____

    _____

Name: _____

Plants Need Water

Have you ever seen a plant that didn't get enough water? Did it look **wilted**? That means it got squishy and started to fall over. Did you know that many plants are made mostly of water? They need water to help them stay up.

Think of a water balloon. If you fill it up with a lot of water, it feels almost hard. It doesn't squish very easily. What happens if you let some of the water out? The balloon gets squishier and softer. That's what happens to plants. If they don't get enough water, they get squishy, soft, and droopy.

Trees don't need as much water to stay up. The wood in their trunks and branches is strong. But, they still need water. If they do not get enough water, their leaves will wilt.

Plants also need water to make food. They have a special green chemical in their leaves. It uses water, sunlight, and air to make food for the plant. The food gives the plant energy so it can grow.

1. What does *wilted* mean?
   a. drooping down   b. standing up   c. making food

2. What three things does a plant need to make food?

   ✔ _____

   ✔ _____

   ✔ _____

3. What are two reasons that plants need water?

   Reason 1: _____

   Reason 2: _____

Name: _____

Plants in Different Places

Different kinds of plants live in different places. They have different ways to get the sunlight, water, and air they need.

Desert

In the desert, there is not much rain. Plants that live in deserts can save water. When it rains, they take up a lot of water through their roots and save it. They have a thick outside layer that holds in the water.

Grasslands

In the grasslands, it only rains part of the year. Grasses can save water and nutrients in their roots to use when it does not rain. This also helps them survive fires. The part of the grass above the ground burns. The part under the ground survives and grows again.

Rainforest

In the rainforest, there are many trees and plants. They grow very close together. It is hard for plants to get enough sunlight on their leaves. So, they grow quickly to reach the top of the forest. Some tilt their leaves to catch the sunlight.

Tundra

In the tundra, it is always cold and sometimes very windy. Plants grow close to the ground. The wind doesn't bother them near the ground. Some are covered in hairy fuzz that keeps them warm. Plants like lichens don't even need soil to grow. They grow on rocks!

1. Which of these is *not* a way that desert plants save water?
   a. They take up a lot of water through their roots.
   b. They grow very close together.
   c. They have a thick outside layer.

2. Grasses that grow in grasslands can survive _____.

3. How do plants in the rainforest get enough sunlight? _____

_____

Name: _____

Plant Life Cycles

All living things have **life cycles**—they grow, they make more living things like themselves, and then they die.

How do plants make more plants like themselves? Plants **reproduce** by making **seeds**. This means that the plants make more plants like themselves. Seeds come from flowers that grow on a plant.

The seeds fall off the plant or are carried away by wind, water, or animals. Sometimes, we plant the seeds ourselves. When a seed ends up in a good place, it will be able to grow a new plant.

What is a good place for a seed to grow? A seed will grow in a place that has what it needs. Most seeds need water, warmth, and air to grow. They need a good place to grow in, like soil. Some seeds need sunlight. Other seeds need darkness.

Under the soil, when everything is just right, the seed breaks open. A **shoot** grows up from the seed. It will become the stem of the plant. The **roots** grow down into the soil. The roots grow bigger. They bring up water and nutrients from the soil to help the plant grow.

The plant grows larger and larger. It grows a lot of **leaves** that make food for the plant. Then, flowers grow on the plant. Seeds form in the flowers. If the seeds get to a place that has what they need, they will make new plants. Then, the life cycle starts all over again!

1. What does *reproduce* mean?
   a. to grow bigger   **b.** to find food   **c.** to make more plants

2. What three things do seeds need to grow?

   _____   _____   _____

3. Use the Word Bank to fill in the missing words.

   A _____ grows up from a seed.

   The _____ grow down.

   The plant grows _____ to make food.

   Flowers form _____ inside.

   The seeds will make _____ plants.

Word Bank
leaves
new
roots
seeds
shoot

Name: _____

Pollination

Plants make seeds to make more plants like themselves. Many plants cannot make seeds by themselves. To **reproduce**, they need help!

The seeds to make new plants are formed in flowers. One part of a flower makes **pollen**. Pollen looks like colored sand. Another part of the flower makes **eggs**. Pollen mixes with an egg to create a seed.

pollen + egg = seed

The pollen cannot make a seed by itself. The egg cannot make a seed by itself. The pollen and the egg need to work together to make a seed.

How does the pollen get from one part of the flower to another?

➡ In some flowers, the pollen just falls down onto the egg part. Plants like these don't need help to make seeds.

➡ Most plants do need help moving their pollen. Who helps them? Animals and bugs called **pollinators** help the plants. Bees, hummingbirds, bats, butterflies, and other animals can all be pollinators.

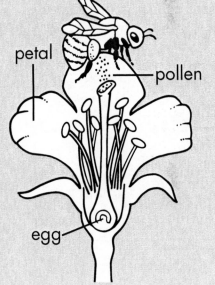

How do pollinators help?

They fly into the flowers. They drink a sweet liquid called **nectar**. Then, pollen sticks to their bodies. When they go to another flower, some of the pollen falls off. It goes into the egg part, and new seeds can be made.

1. Which part of a plant makes seeds?
   a. leaves
   b. flowers
   c. roots

2. Pollen needs to combine with an _____ to make a seed.

3. What do *pollinators* do? _____

_____

Name: _____

Seed Dispersal: Wind and Water

If a seed falls off a plant, it might grow a new plant right where it falls. But, if many seeds grow under the plant, they will be very close together. The young plants will probably not get enough sunlight or water. It is better for plants when they spread out. They need to grow in new places. When seeds move away from their parent plant, scientists say they **disperse**. How do seeds disperse? Sometimes, they get help from wind or water.

Wind

Some seeds can travel with help from the wind.

➡ Dandelion seeds have little parachutes attached. They can fly a long way in the wind.

➡ Cottonwood seeds are surrounded by fluff to help them move in the air.

➡ Maple seeds have wings that make them spin around. This keeps them in the air longer so the wind can move them to a new place.

Water

Water helps some seeds travel.

➡ The seeds of a coconut tree are very large, but they can float. They have thick shells to keep the salt water out. Coconuts can float across entire oceans and grow very far from their parent tree.

➡ Alder trees grow best by rivers. Alder seeds fall into the river and float away. If they land on the shore, they will grow.

1. What does *disperse* mean?
   a. to blow in the wind   **b.** to grow into plants   **c.** to move away

2. Why do seeds need to disperse? _____

_____

3. Write about one way that seeds disperse by either water or wind.

_____

_____

Name: _____

Seed Dispersal: Animals

Seeds have a better chance to grow when they move away from their parent plant. Scientists say that seeds **disperse**. How do seeds disperse? Sometimes, they get help from animals.

Some animals are messy eaters. They take fruit off the plant. They carry the fruit with them to another place. When they eat the fruit, they drop some of the seeds. The seeds might grow in the new place.

Animals such as squirrels and blue jays hide food to eat later. They don't always remember where they hid their nuts and seeds. Some of the nuts and seeds can grow where they are hidden.

Some kinds of seeds have hooks or sticky parts. When an animal comes close, the seeds stick to the animal's fur. The animal travels to a new place, and the seeds fall off. The seeds can grow in a new place.

Sometimes, animals eat fruits and swallow the seeds. Then they walk, crawl, or fly to another place. The seeds travel through the animal's body and come out again. If the seeds fall in a good place, they can still grow!

1. Which is not a way that seeds *disperse*?
    a. animals carry them
    b. animals eat them
    c. animals throw them

2. How do you think sweet fruit around a plant's seeds can help the seeds *disperse*?

    _____

    _____

3. How does a seed with small hooks get *dispersed*?

    _____

    _____

Name: _____

Seed Dispersal: People

When seeds move away from their parent plant, they have a better chance to grow. Scientists say they **disperse**. How do seeds disperse? Sometimes, they disperse with some help from people.

People can accidentally move seeds. If you walk in tall grass, you might find seeds stuck to your socks, your pants, or even in your hair. These seeds take a ride on you and can fall off as you walk. They might fall off in a new place where the seeds can grow.

Seeds can take a ride with people in other ways, too. They can get into cars, boats, or even airplanes and move to a new place. Seeds can hide in things that humans move, like soil or food.

People also help plants disperse on purpose. Farmers plant seeds in fields. People plant seeds in pots and in gardens. People make sure the seeds get what they need to grow. Seeds need sunlight, water, and nutrients. The seeds grow where people plant them. When people plant seeds and help them grow, it is called **cultivation**.

1. People help plants *disperse* _____.
   a. accidentally
   b. on purpose
   c. both **a** and **b**

2. What is *cultivation*? _____

   _____

3. Do you think plants are more likely to grow when people disperse them accidentally or on purpose? Why do you think so? What is your evidence?

   _____

   _____

   _____

Name: _____

Plant Defenses

Plants can't run away from animals that want to eat them. So, how do they **defend** themselves?

Sharp Parts

Many plants have sharp parts. When an animal takes a bite of one of these plants, it gets a big surprise. Ouch! A plant can have pointy parts on its branches or stems. These are called *thorns*. Plants like cacti have needle-like spines. An animal that takes a bite from one of these plants will not like it. It won't try to eat from that plant again.

Poisons

Many plants are **poisonous**. They have chemicals in them that make animals sick. The poison can be inside the leaves. When an animal eats the plant, it gets sick. The poison might be on little hairs on the plant. These hairs can hurt an animal if it touches them.

Animals and Plants Work Together

Some plants work together with bugs. Acacia trees are good places for ants to live. The ants help the tree. They bite and sting animals that come to eat the leaves!

1. What does *defend* mean?
   a. sharp parts   **b.** to protect from enemies   **c.** to work in groups

2. Write two ways a plant can *defend* itself.

   _____   _____

3. How does having thorns help some plants?

   _____

   _____

Name: _____

Plants That Eat Meat

Plants can make their own food. But some very special plants can eat animals! They are called **carnivorous** plants. This means they eat meat.

Plants need nutrients (food) to grow. Most of the time, plants get nutrients from the soil. But some plants live where the soil doesn't have enough nutrients. These plants get their nutrients by **digesting** (eating) bugs and even small mice and frogs!

The Venus flytrap has pairs of flat leaves. They can open and close. When a bug goes in between the leaves, the plant snaps the leaves shut. The bug is trapped! The plant uses chemicals to dissolve the bug. In a couple of days, there is nothing left of the bug but its shell. The trap opens, and the shell falls out. The Venus flytrap is ready to catch another bug.

Pitcher plants also catch bugs. These plants have really interesting leaves. The bottom part of the leaf makes a deep bowl. This is the trap. Bugs like to eat the sweet nectar around the outside of the bowl. As they reach for more nectar, they fall into the trap! They drown in the sticky liquid, and the plant **digests** their bodies.

1. What can *carnivorous* plants do that other plants can't?
   a. eat meat   **b.** protect themselves from enemies   **c.** open and close

2. Write two ways a *carnivorous* plant can catch prey.

   _____

   _____

3. Why do *carnivorous* plants eat meat?

   _____

   _____

Name: _____

Record-Breaking Plants

Have you ever wondered what the oldest or biggest plants in the world are? Read on to find out!

Oldest Trees
The oldest trees in the world are bristlecone pines. They grow high up on the sides of mountains. These trees can live over 3,000 years.

Largest Flower
The world's largest flower is the stinking corpse lily. It can grow to almost five feet across. It weighs as much as a two-year-old child. It is also the world's smelliest flower. It smells like dead animals.

Heaviest Fruit
The Atlantic Giant Pumpkin is the heaviest fruit. One pumpkin can weigh over 2,000 pounds. That's as much as a small car!

Fastest-Growing Plant
Bamboo is the fastest-growing plant. Some kinds can grow up to 35 inches each day. That means they grow almost an inch and a half every hour.

Slowest-Growing Plant
A saguaro cactus grows slowly. It can take 10 years for one cactus to grow from a seed to one inch tall. It won't grow a flower until it is 35 years old. And, it can take 100 years for the first arm to grow!

1. Where do bristlecone pines grow?
   a. on a farm   **b.** in a desert   **c.** on the sides of mountains

2. If a bamboo plant grows 35 inches in one day, how much will it grow in two days?

   Do the math!

3. Which of the record-breaking plants would you like to learn more about?

_____

Name: _____

The School Garden

Mrs. Jones's class was very excited. Today, they would plant their new school garden! Where should they plant the garden? Not in the shade. Plants need lots of sunlight. The class chose a sunny spot for their plants.

First, the students cleared and raked the garden area. They took out the trash and pulled the weeds. Plants need good soil to grow, so Mrs. Jones brought big bags of soil. The students used shovels to spread the soil all around the garden.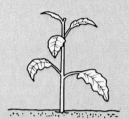

Mrs. Jones gave each student a small plant. "What kind of plants are these?" the students asked. Mrs. Jones smiled. "It will be a surprise," she said.

The students dug little holes in the soil and carefully put the small plants into the holes. The roots go under the soil. The stem and leaves stand above the soil.

Then, the students filled watering cans with a hose. They poured water around each plant and let it soak into the soil. They were careful not to pour too much water.

Every day, the class went to take care of the garden. They watered the plants and pulled out the weeds. The plants grew bigger and bigger.

One day, the students got a big surprise. The plants had small, round fruits growing on them. Every day, the fruits got bigger. They turned red.

Then the students knew what kind of plants they had planted in their garden.

They were tomatoes!

1. What did the students give their plants to help them grow?
    a. sunlight, soil, and water
    b. sunlight, roots, and water
    c. shade, water, and soil

2. Why did the students plant their garden in a sunny spot? _____

_____

3. How did the students care for their plants? _____

_____

Name: _____

Design a Plant

Directions

1. In the box below, make up and draw a new plant that no one has ever seen before.

2. Include the things that a plant must have to grow and reproduce.

3. Check each part off as you label it on your drawing.

4. Be sure to color your plant!

| ❑ roots | ❑ leaves | ❑ fruit |
| ❑ stem | ❑ flower | ❑ seeds |

Name: _____

What Animals Need

Survive means to stay alive. Animals need some things to survive. They will die without these things.

What do animals need to survive? They need oxygen, water, food, and shelter.

All animals need oxygen. Most animals get oxygen from the air they breathe. Underwater animals get it from the water. Animals must also drink water and eat food to survive. Most animals need **shelter**. A shelter protects an animal. A shelter is a place for the animal to keep warm or cool.

You need oxygen (air), water, food, and shelter to survive. How do you get what you need?

➡ You get *food* from a store, or your family might grow some food.

➡ You can get *water* from a sink or a shower.

➡ You find *shelter* in a building, such as a house, an apartment, or a school.

Can animals find the things they need in the same ways? No, they cannot. Animals must find what they need in the space around them. They can't go to a store to buy food. They don't get water from sinks. Animals must live in a place where they can find what they need to survive.

1. What does *survive* mean?
   a. to stay alive   **b.** a safe place   **c.** the space around an animal

2. To *survive*, animals need _____, _____,

   _____, and _____.

3. Write how you get what you need to *survive*.

   Food: _____

   Oxygen: _____

   Shelter: _____

   Water: _____

Name: _____

Animals Need Oxygen

All animals need **oxygen**. It is found in air and in water. You can't see oxygen and you can't smell it, but it is very important. Animals need oxygen to live.

Take a deep breath. What do you feel? When you breathe in, your lungs fill with air. Your body takes oxygen from the air. It sends oxygen through your blood to all the parts of your body.

Now breathe out. When you breathe out, you get rid of the part of the air that you don't need.

Like you, all animals need oxygen to survive. Oxygen inside an animal's body helps turn food into energy. Animals need energy to grow and survive.

Land animals breathe air into their lungs like you do. Some animals, such as frogs, can take in air through their skin. These animals get oxygen from the air.

Underwater animals breathe water into their gills. They get oxygen from the water.

Some animals may surprise you. Whales and dolphins live in the water. They look like fish. But they do not get their oxygen from the water. They must come up to the top of the water. They breathe air through a hole in the top of their heads!

1. Land animals breathe air to get *oxygen*. What body parts do they use?
   a. gills   **b.** lungs   **c.** skin

2. Animals with gills get *oxygen* from the _____ they live in.

3. Why do animals need *oxygen* to survive? _____

_____

Name: _____

Animals Need Water

All animals need water to survive. Their bodies use water in lots of ways:

➡ Water helps keep animals from getting too hot.

➡ Water helps remove waste from animal bodies.

➡ Animal bodies use water to get energy from food. They need energy to grow and to move.

➡ Some animals, such as fish and whales, need water to live in. They can't live without it. Their bodies would dry out, and they would die.

All animals have a lot of water in their bodies. How do they get water? They drink it. They also get water from the food they eat. Some animals live in places where there isn't very much water. They get all their water from the food they eat.

Did you know that your body is made mostly of water? Yes, it is. There is more water in your body than anything else!

1. Animal bodies use water and oxygen to get _____ from food.
   a. blood   **b.** energy   **c.** waste

2. What are two ways animals get water?

   _____

   _____

3. Think about the way you get water and the way animals get water. How are they different?

   _____

   _____

   _____

Name: _____

Animals Need Food

All animals need energy. Animals get energy when they eat food. Without energy, an animal would die. It helps them grow, move, and protect themselves. Animals cannot make their own energy. How do they get it?

➡ Some animals eat plants for food.

➡ Some animals eat other animals.

➡ Some animals eat both plants and other animals.

Much of the energy on Earth comes from the Sun. Plants use the Sun's energy to make food so they can grow. Animals eat plants or other animals so they can grow. In this way, all animals get their energy from the Sun.

1. The Sun shines on the grass. The grass uses the Sun's energy to grow.

2. The rabbit eats the grass. It gets energy from the grass.

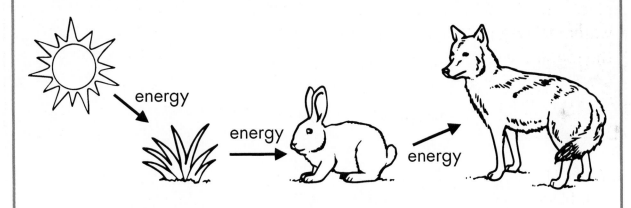

3. The coyote eats the rabbit. It gets energy from the rabbit.

Directions: Look at the pictures below. Draw arrows showing how the energy from the Sun gets to the plants and animals.

Name: _____

Animals Need Shelter

Animals need **shelter**. Shelter means a safe place to hide or rest.

Some animals need shelter to keep them safe from weather. A shelter might keep them cool in hot weather or warm in cold weather.

Some animals need shelter to keep them safe from predators. A shelter might be a place that is too small for a predator to get into. Or, it might be a place that is too high up for a predator to reach.

Some animals find shelter in the space around them.

➡ Some birds use holes in tree trunks for shelter and nesting.

➡ Clownfish find shelter in another animal called an *anemone*.

➡ Some owls use holes in the ground that are dug by prairie dogs.

Some animals make their own shelter.

➡ Birds build nests in trees or on cliffs using things they find, such as sticks or mud.

➡ Some ants dig tunnels or build giant hills out of mud and dirt.

➡ Bees and wasps build hives.

➡ Beavers build dams on streams using sticks and logs.

1. What is *shelter*?   **a.** cold weather   **b.** a predator   **c.** a safe place

2. What are two reasons an animal might need *shelter*?

_____

_____

3. What are some places where you find *shelter*?

_____

How do they help you? _____

_____

Name: _____

What Is a Habitat?

A **habitat** is the area where an animal lives. It is a place that has what the animal needs. It has food, shelter, and water. People can live almost anywhere because we can move around and buy or build the things we need.

How do we get food and shelter?

Most of the time, ships, trains, and trucks move food from where it is grown to a store where we can buy it.

We build homes, schools, and other buildings for shelter.

If it gets cold, we can turn on a heater to stay warm. We can buy warm jackets and blankets.

How do we get water?

Pipes bring water into our homes and schools.

Animals can't buy or move things. They need to live in a place where they can find what they need to survive. Here are some examples:

➡ Sharks need to live in water where there are fish to eat. They cannot get fish at a store!

➡ Bears need to live where they can find caves or dens to stay warm for the winter. They cannot use wood, hammers, and nails to build houses.

➡ Koalas can only eat the leaves of one kind of tree, so they must live where that kind of tree grows. They cannot drive cars or ride on trains to get to the trees they need.

1. What is a *habitat*?
   a. a place that has what an animal needs
   b. a place where fish live
   c. a place where trees grow

2. A *habitat* provides _____, _____, and water.

3. What are some animals that live in your neighborhood?

   _____   _____

   How do they get what they need? _____

   _____

Name: _____

Living and Nonliving Parts of Habitats

Animals must find what they need in their habitat. Some of the things they need are other **living** things.

Animals eat living things. Some eat plants. Some eat other animals. Some eat both plants and animals. Some animals use living things for their shelter. They can use trees or bushes.

Animals need **nonliving** things, too. They need to breathe air or water. Many animals use nonliving things for shelter. Some live in holes in the ground. Other animals live in cracks in cliffs. Some live in caves.

Water and sunlight are also important nonliving things. There would be no plants and no food without the Sun and water.

Directions: Look at the picture of each habitat. List the living and nonliving things in the habitat.

1.

Living

_____

_____

Nonliving

_____

_____

2.

Living

_____

_____

Nonliving

_____

_____

Name: _____

Omnivores Have Options

Imagine that you can only eat pizza. You can't survive on anything else. Where could you live? You could only live in places where there is pizza!

Now, think about all the things you really eat. You can eat fruits and vegetables, bread, and lots of other things. Can you live in places where there is no pizza? Yes! You can find food in lots of places.

Animals that eat both plants and meat are called **omnivores**. They can eat many kinds of food in their habitats. If they can't find one food, they can eat something else. Omnivores have a better chance of survival than animals that can only eat one kind of food.

Bears are omnivores. They can eat lots of different things. One of their favorite foods is fish. They can also eat other kinds of meat, such as small animals and insects. Bears also eat plants, such as roots, berries, and flowers. If there aren't enough fish to eat, bears can eat other things in their habitat.

1. What is an *omnivore*?
    a. an animal that has two parents
    b. an animal that eats both plants and meat
    c. an animal that lives in the forest

2. *Omnivores* have a better chance of _____ than animals that only eat one kind of food.

3. Why do *omnivores* have a better chance of survival?

    _____

    _____

    _____

Name: _____

Wet or Dry?

Water is an important part of animal habitats. All animals need water to live.

Rainforest

Rainforests are wet and warm. Rain falls all year long. A lot of water means there are many kinds of plants and animals. Monkeys, frogs, and birds live high up in the tall trees. Jaguars, anteaters, and ants live on the shady ground under the trees.

Desert

Deserts do not get very much rain. It is hard to live in a dry desert. There are fewer kinds of plants and animals. Desert animals get most of the water they need from their food. Desert plants, like cacti, store water in their leaves, stems, or roots.

Ocean

Many different animals live in the ocean. Sharks and other fish live underwater. They have gills to take oxygen from the water. They cannot breathe air. They will die if they are not in the water.

Some animals live in water but have lungs to breathe air. Whales and dolphins live in the water. They must swim to the top to breathe air. Seals, walruses, and otters can go on land, but they find their food in the water.

1. The _____ gets a lot of rain, and many kinds of plants and animals live there.

    a. desert   **b.** ocean   **c.** rainforest

2. Animals that live in deserts get most of their water from _____.

3. Choose one ocean animal, and explain how it gets oxygen. _____

_____

_____

Name: _____

Migration

Some animals don't stay in the same habitat all year. In summer, they live where it is warm. They have plenty of food. It is safe to have babies. When it gets cold in winter, they leave. They go to a warmer habitat where they can find more food. Moving from one habitat to another is called **migrating**.

Whales migrate in the ocean. They swim to warmer waters in the winter. They have babies. The babies grow bigger and stronger. Then, whale families swim to colder water where there is more food.

Sperm whales

Zebras

Zebras in Africa migrate. They live on the plains and eat grass. When the weather gets hot and there is no rain, they start walking. They walk to find green grass and water. Sometimes they have to walk hundreds of miles!

Birds called Arctic terns migrate farther than any other animal. Half the year, they live near the top of Earth. They eat fish. They build nests and raise their babies. When it gets colder, they fly to the other end of Earth. They migrate 44,000 miles!

Arctic tern

1. What does the word *migrate* mean?
   a. to move across the forest floor
   b. to move from one nest to another
   c. to move from one habitat to another

2. Name three animals that migrate.

   _____ _____ _____

   Do you know of an animal that migrates in your neighborhood? If so, what animal is it? _____

3. Animals migrate to stay _____ and find _____.

Name: _____

Mammals

What do you have in common with a whale? How are you the same as a mouse? You are a **mammal**!

Mammals are animals that have all these things in common:

Mammals are warm-blooded. This means that their bodies can use some of the energy they get from food to make themselves warmer. They don't need the Sun to make them warm. Mammals can also cool off by sweating or panting. Mammals can live in lots of places. Seals live in cold ocean waters. Rabbits can live in the hot desert.

Mammals have hair. Sometimes, the hair covers the whole body. We call that **fur**. Dogs and bears have fur. Sometimes, the hair is very short or there are just a few hairs. Hippos have just a few hairs. The hairs are around their mouths and ears and on the tips of their tails.

Mammals drink milk from their mothers. When mammal babies are born, they cannot eat regular food. They must drink milk from their mothers for a while. Their mothers take care of them until they can eat food on their own.

There are many kinds of mammals. They can be very big, very small, or any size in between. They can walk, swim, and fly. Some mammals eat plants, and some eat other animals. Some eat both plants and meat. Mammals can live in almost any habitat. Humans are mammals, too.

1. A *warm-blooded* animal is an animal that _____.
   - **a.** can swim in oceans or lakes
   - **b.** can make itself warmer or cooler
   - **c.** gets its warmth from the Sun

2. Mammals drink _____ from their mothers after they are born.

3. How do you know that you are a *mammal*? What is your evidence?

_____

_____

Name: _____

Birds

What makes birds different from other animals? Birds are warm-blooded and have spines. Mammals have both of those things, too. Birds lay eggs. But so do some reptiles. Birds have wings. But some insects do, too.

So, what do only birds have? Birds are the only animals with feathers. Feathers are made of keratin. It's the same thing that makes your hair and fingernails.

Like mammals' hair, feathers can keep a bird warm or cool. Feathers can also keep water off of a bird's body. And, feathers are a must for flying!

Ostrich and her chicks

Gull

All birds have wings, but not all birds can fly. Some large birds, such as ostriches and emus, are very fast runners. They hold their wings out when they run to help them balance. Penguins are great swimmers. They use their wings as flippers.

1. What do only birds have?
   a. hair
   b. scales
   c. feathers

2. Penguins can _____ instead of fly.

3. How do feathers help a bird survive?

_____

_____

_____

Name: _____

Reptiles

Reptiles are cold-blooded. This means that their bodies can't warm or cool themselves. If the weather is cold, they must lie in the sunlight to get warm. They can't sweat or pant. If the weather is hot, they move into shade or bury themselves to keep cool.

Iguana

Reptiles have dry, scaly skin. It helps keep them from drying out so they can live in dry places. Scaly skin does not stretch or grow with an animal like your skin does. Most reptiles must shed their skin once it gets too small. There is a new, bigger skin underneath.

Some reptiles lay eggs, and some have live babies. For all reptiles, their babies look like small versions of the adults. Baby turtles look like small adult turtles. Baby snakes look like tiny adult snakes.

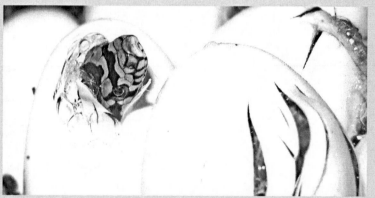
Snake hatching

1. What does it mean if an animal is *cold-blooded*?
   a. It has scaly skin and no fur.
   b. It is mean to other animals.
   c. It cannot make itself warmer or cooler.

2. Reptile babies look like _____ reptiles.

3. Why must reptiles shed their skins?

   _____

   _____

Name: _____

Amphibians

The word **amphibian** means "two lives." These animals start life looking one way. As they grow, they change a lot! Frogs and salamanders lay their eggs in water. The babies have gills and tails. They live in the water while they grow. Soon, they grow legs, and then lungs. Then, they come out of the water and live on land.

Tadpole with tail and legs

Adult amphibians breathe air into their lungs. They also breathe and get water through their smooth skin. Their bodies make sticky, wet stuff called **mucus** that helps keep their skin wet. They cannot spend too much time in the sunlight or in the wind. They will dry out, and they will not be able to breathe. They will die.

Frog

Frogs and salamanders must live in or near water. Toads can live in places that are drier. But, they must keep their skin moist. Toads bury themselves in the ground during the hot part of the day.

Amphibians will eat any small animal they can catch. They will eat insects, spiders, slugs, snails, and worms. Amphibians do not have teeth. They catch their prey with their sticky tongues and swallow them whole.

1. Why do amphibians have *mucus*?
   a. because they have a cold
   b. because their skin must be wet
   c. because they live in water

2. *Amphibians* breathe air through their _____

   and _____.

3. How do *amphibians* eat?

   _____

   _____

Name: _____

Fish

Fish are animals that *only* live in water. They have gills instead of lungs. They cannot survive out of the water.

Fish have **scales** on their bodies. Fish scales are made of keratin. It's the same thing that makes your hair and fingernails. The scales are not connected to each other, so they can slide next to each other as the fish moves. Scales protect the fish's body. Some kinds of fish scales get bigger as the fish grows. Other fish grow more scales as they get bigger. If a fish loses a scale, it will grow back.

There are many different kinds and sizes of fish. The biggest fish is the whale shark. It is not a whale. It is a very big shark. Whale sharks can be as big as three cars. The smallest fish in the world is just ¼-inch long. It could fit on your fingernail!

Whale shark

Some fish live in salt water in the oceans. Other fish live in fresh water in streams, rivers, lakes, and ponds.

Dolphins and whales are NOT fish! They are mammals that live in the water. They have lungs and must come up to the top of the water to breathe air.

1. Which of these things is not true about fish *scales*?
   a. If a fish loses a scale, it will grow back.
   b. Fish scales are made of the same thing as your hair and fingernails.
   c. Fish shed their scales when they grow.

2. Some fish live in _____ water, and some live in salt water.

3. Why must fish live in water?

   _____

   _____

   _____

Name: _____

Insects

Have you ever seen an ant or a fly? Then you have seen an insect! Insects are everywhere. There are more insects on Earth than any other kind of animal.

Exoskeleton

Your skeleton is on the inside of your body. It holds you up. It keeps you from being a puddle of squishy stuff.

An insect's skeleton is on the outside. It is called an **exoskeleton**. *Exo* means "outside." It's like a shell that covers the whole body. It holds the insect together. It protects the soft body inside.

Ant

Wings

Some insects have wings. They are very different from bird wings. Insect wings are part of their exoskeletons. Insect wings do not have feathers like bird wings. Birds have two wings. Insects usually have four wings.

Compound Eyes

Insects have compound eyes. Their eyes don't see just one view of the world like our eyes do. They have a lot of little eyes, all seeing at the same time. They can see above them, below them, all around them, and even behind them. This is why it is hard to catch a fly!

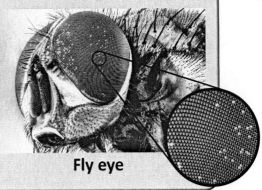

Fly eye

1. An *exoskeleton* is _____.
  a. a puddle of squishy stuff
  b. bones on the inside of a body
  c. a hard covering on the outside

2. There are more _____ than any other kind of animal.

3. How are insect wings different from bird wings?

_____

_____

_____

Name: _____

Insect Body Parts

Insect bodies are very different from your body. An insect has three main body parts.

- The **head** is at the front. The eyes, mouth, and antennae are on the head.
- The **thorax** is in the middle. All insects have six legs. The legs are attached to the thorax. If the insect has wings, they are attached to the thorax.
- The **abdomen** is at the back. The insect's heart is in the abdomen.

Directions: Use the Word Bank to label the insect body parts.

Word Bank	abdomen	antennae	eyes
	head	legs	thorax

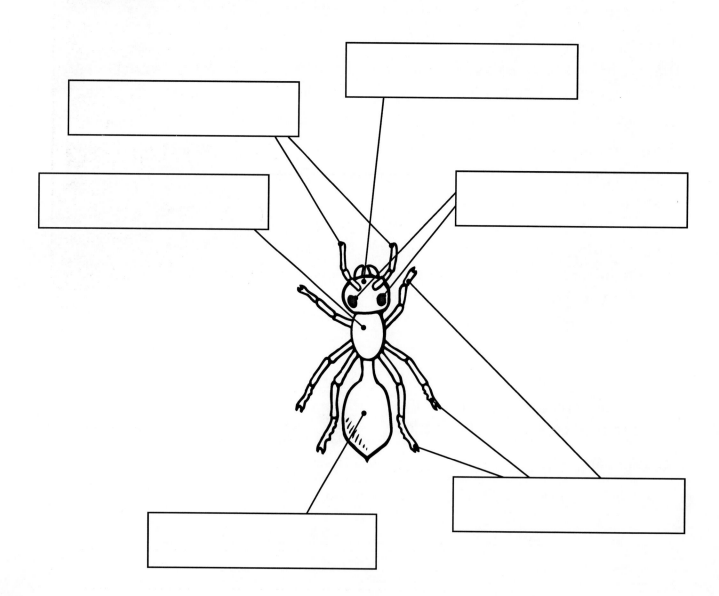

Name: _____

Arachnids

Have you ever seen a spider? Most spiders are small. They look like insects, but they are not insects! They are called **arachnids**.

Arachnids are animals with eight legs. Spiders and scorpions are arachnids. They can be found anywhere on land. Some arachnids even live in the water.

Arachnids have an exoskeleton like insects. But, arachnids only have two body parts. They have eight legs. They do not have wings or antennae.

Arachnids are predators. That means they hunt other animals. Some spiders make a web to catch prey. Some make a trap, and some jump on their prey.

Wasp spider

The next time you see a small animal crawling, count the legs. If it has six legs, it is an insect. If it has eight legs, it is an arachnid.

1. Spiders and _____ are *arachnids*.
   a. insects
   b. ants
   c. scorpions

2. *Arachnids* have _____ legs and _____ body parts.

3. How are *arachnids* different from insects?

   _____

   _____

   _____

Name: _____

Crustaceans

Have you ever seen a pill bug? Some people call them roly-poly bugs or sow bugs. They have many legs. Pill bugs can curl up into a ball. They live in dark, cool places.

Pill bugs are not bugs. They are **crustaceans** that live on land. Crabs and shrimp are crustaceans that live in water. Crustaceans are like insects and arachnids. They have an **exoskeleton**. It has an extra layer that makes it harder and heavier. That is why a pill bug looks like it is wearing armor. It has a strong exoskeleton!

Fun facts about crustaceans:

- Lobsters and pill bugs have blue blood.
- Crayfish swim backward and walk forward.
- Coconut crabs are very big. They can live to be 60 years old!

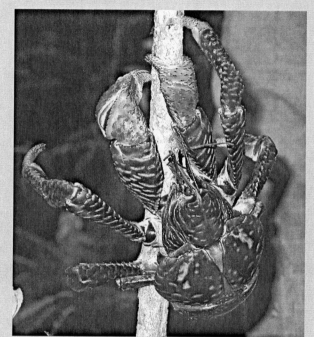

Coconut crab climbing a stick

1. Pill bugs are _____.
   a. crustaceans
   b. arachnids
   c. insects

2. A *crustacean* has a heavy, hard _____.

3. Why do you think pill bugs curl up into a ball?

   _____

   _____

   _____

Name: _____

Gastropods

Not all crawling animals are bugs. Snails are not bugs. Snails are **gastropods**. They do not have any bones. They do not have any legs. Each snail slides along on one big, squishy foot.

Some gastropods have shells, and some do not. Some gastropods live in water, and some live on land.

Nudibranch

- **Snails** are gastropods that have shells.
- **Slugs** are gastropods that do *not* have shells.
- **Nudibranchs** are slugs that live in the ocean. They have very bright colors. Their colors warn predators not to eat them. Nudibranchs are pretty and poisonous!

Gastropods have a strange way of eating. Most gastropods eat with a **radula**. It is like a tongue covered with tiny teeth. They scrape their radula on their food. It looks like they are licking their food. The radula rips the food into tiny pieces.

Giant African land snail

Some gastropods are very big. The giant African land snail can be as big as a shoe.

And some gastropods are very small. Mud snails are so small that it is hard to see them!

1. Slugs are different from snails because they do not have _____.
   a. legs   **b.** shells   **c.** bones

2. A *nudibranch's* bright colors warn predators that it is _____.

3. How do *gastropods* eat with a *radula*?

   _____

   _____

Name: _____

What Are Seasons?

Did you know that Earth is tilted? It is! As Earth spins around, sometimes the place where you live leans toward the Sun, and sometimes it leans away. This is the reason we have seasons.

In summer, the place you live is tilted toward the Sun. The Sun shines right down on you, and it shines for a longer time each day. The weather feels hotter.

In winter, the place you live is tilted away from the Sun. The Sun still shines, but it is lower in the sky. The Sun doesn't shine for as long each day. The weather feels colder.

Winter

Summer

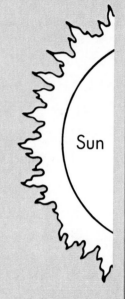

Sun

You can see the way seasons change by looking at trees.

➡ In summer, it is warm. The trees have lots of leaves.

➡ In fall, it gets cooler. The leaves change color and fall off the tree.

➡ In winter, it is cold. The trees have no leaves.

➡ In spring, it gets warmer. The leaves grow back, and flowers bloom.

Directions: Label each tree with a season.

Word Bank	fall	spring	summer	winter

_____   _____   _____   _____

Name: _____

Summer

Summer is the season when the days are longest. In the Northern Hemisphere, summer starts in June. It ends in September. The Sun shines brightly, and the weather is warm. Plants grow quickly, and animals can find plenty of food.

In some places, the summer is very hot. People wear short-sleeved shirts and shorts or sundresses. They go swimming and eat ice cream to cool off. Summer is a good time for picnics in the park.

For some kids, there is no school in the summer. They go on vacations with their families. They might go to the beach or a lake. Some families go camping. They sleep in tents and have campfires.

In some places, summer brings thunderstorms. Big, black clouds blow across the sky. Heavy rain and hail fall. There is thunder and lightning. Stay safe by staying indoors during a storm!

1. What activity would be best in the summer?
   a. sledding down a snowy hill
   b. building a snowman
   c. going swimming

2. Summer is the season when the days are _____.

3. What do you like to do in the summer?

   _____

   _____

Name: _____

Fall

Fall comes after summer. The fall months are September, October, and November in the Northern Hemisphere. The days get shorter. The weather gets cooler. Leaves on the trees turn brown, yellow, orange, and red. Animals start to get ready for winter. Squirrels gather acorns. Some birds fly to warmer places.

In fall, you wear warmer clothes, such as long-sleeved shirts and sweaters. You might go on a hayride. You can pick out a pumpkin in a pumpkin patch. Farmers gather apples, squash, and corn. It is fun to go for a walk and look at all the fall colors.

Many kids go back to school in fall. You might miss summer vacation, but it is fun to see all your friends again!

1. Fall comes after _____.
   a. spring   b. summer   c. winter

2. In fall, the days get _____, and the weather gets

   _____.

3. What is your favorite thing to do in the fall?

   _____

   _____

   _____

Name: _____

Winter

Winter is the coldest season. December, January, and February are winter months in the Northern Hemisphere.

In some places, it snows. Bears and skunks sleep through the cold winter in their dens. You can make a snowman or go sledding. Ponds freeze, and you can skate on the ice. You must wear warm clothes. Bundle up in a heavy jacket, scarf, hat, and snow boots. Do you like to drink hot chocolate in winter?

In some places, it does not snow in winter, but it is colder than usual. The rain comes and helps plants grow. It can be very cold at night.

Many people celebrate winter holidays. It is a time for families to get together. They eat special foods and play games. Some people light candles or give one another gifts.

1. Winter is the _____ season.
    a. coldest   **b.** warmest   **c.** shortest

2. Some animals _____ through the cold winter.

3. What is winter weather like where you live? What do you like to do?

_____

_____

_____

_____

Name: _____

Spring

Spring comes after winter. It starts in March and ends in May in the Northern Hemisphere.

In spring, the days get longer, and there is more sunshine. Plants start to grow again. Spring rain helps the plants grow and grow. Animals that slept through the winter come out. Many baby animals are born in spring.

When it rains in spring, you can wear a raincoat, a hat, and boots. It is fun to jump in puddles!

Many schools have spring break. Some families go on vacation. Some people stay home and relax. Spring is a nice time to go for a walk, and look for flowers blooming. You can enjoy watching the birds. You might even see some baby animals! Just remember to take a coat because it often rains in spring.

1. Spring is _____ than winter.
   a. colder   **b.** warmer   **c.** darker

2. In spring, the days get _____ and there is more

   _____.

3. What do you like to do in the spring?

   _____

   _____

   _____

Name: _____

What Is Weather?

What is the weather like outside today? Is it rainy or sunny? Are there clouds in the sky?

Weather is what is going on in the sky and the air. These are the things that make up weather:

Air temperature is a measure of how hot or cold the air is.

➡ A low temperature means it is cold.

➡ A high temperature means it is hot.

Clouds are made of tiny droplets of water. Clouds look soft and fluffy, but they are really just wet.

➡ Have you ever been in fog? *Fog* is a cloud on the ground!

Precipitation is water that falls from clouds.

➡ It might be *rain*, or if it is really cold, it might be *hail* or *snow*.

Wind is moving air. You can't see wind, but you can feel it. Wind moves clouds from one place to another, which makes the weather change.

➡ If the air outside moves slowly, we say there is a *breeze* or a light wind.

➡ If the air outside moves quickly, we say it is *windy*.

➡ Really fast wind can be dangerous. It can knock down trees and power lines.

1. What is *air temperature*?
   a. air moving very fast
   b. a measure of how hot or cold the air is
   c. water that falls from clouds

2. Clouds are made of _____.

3. What are some things that you have seen wind do?

   _____

   _____

   _____

Name: _____

Weather Reports

Thermometer

Before you get dressed in the morning, you should check the weather report. It will tell you what the weather will be today. Then, you will know what to wear. If the weather report says it will rain, bring your raincoat. If the weather report says it will be sunny and hot, wear short sleeves.

People who predict the weather use many tools.

- A **thermometer** tells how hot or cold the air is.

- A **wind vane** tells what direction the wind is blowing. That helps us know how the clouds are moving.

- A **rain gauge** measures how much rain has fallen.

Sunday		Monday		Tuesday		Wednesday	
81°	51°	70°	53°	79°	52°	67°	53°
High	Low	High	Low	High	Low	High	Low

Weather reports can help us stay safe. If there is a big storm coming, we can get ready. We can stay indoors. Weather can change quickly. It might be sunny in the morning but stormy in the afternoon!

1. A *thermometer* tells _____.
   a. how much rain has fallen
   b. which direction the wind is blowing
   c. how hot or cold the air is

2. What is the weather like today where you live?

   _____

   _____

3. What is your favorite kind of weather? Why?

   _____

   _____

Name: _____

Reading a Weather Report

These are the different kinds of weather you might see in a weather report:

 Sunny weather means there are very few clouds. The Sun shines brightly. It will be a good day to go outside, but be sure to wear sunscreen.

 Partly cloudy means there will be some clouds in the sky. It might be sunny part of the day, but clouds will block the Sun, too.

 Cloudy means there will be lots of clouds in the sky. You will not see sunshine on a cloudy day.

 Windy means the wind will be blowing. Wind moves the trees and blows leaves across the ground.

 Rainy means there are clouds coming that are full of water. Rain will fall from the clouds, so bring your umbrella!

 Stormy means it will be windy and rainy. There might be lightning and thunder.

✳ ✳ ✳
✳ ✳ **Snowy** means snow will fall from the clouds. It will be cold outside. You will need warm clothes.

Directions: Read the weather report below. Answer the questions.

Monday	75 degrees	Partly Cloudy	
Tuesday	66 degrees	Rainy	
Wednesday	78 degrees	Sunny	
Thursday	79 degrees	Windy	
Friday	80 degrees	Sunny	

1. What does the weather report say the weather will be like on Monday?

_____

2. Which day would be best for flying a kite? _____

3. On what day will you need your umbrella? _____

Name: _____

Dangerous Weather

Some kinds of weather can be dangerous. We need to get ready and be careful in dangerous weather.

Strong **storms** can bring a lot of rain. The wind blows hard, and there might be lightning. Sometimes, big hailstones fall.

A **hurricane** is a storm so big it can cover a whole state. Hurricanes bring very strong wind and rain. They can make the ocean waves come very far up on the land.

Blizzards bring a lot of snow and wind. It is hard to see during a blizzard because of all the snow in the air.

If too much rain falls all at once, it can cause a **flood**. Water starts to flow out of rivers and streams. It runs into towns and cities. It can get into buildings. It can even carry cars away.

When we know that dangerous weather is coming, we can get ready. We should stay indoors during big storms or blizzards. If there is a hurricane coming, sometimes people need to leave and go somewhere safe.

1. If too much rain falls all at once, it can cause a _____.
   a. blizzard **b.** flood **c.** hailstorm

2. Name three kinds of dangerous weather.

   _____ _____ _____

3. What kinds of dangerous weather happen where you live? How do you stay safe?

   _____

   _____

   _____

Name: _____

Rainbows

Have you ever seen a rainbow? The pretty colors stretch across the sky. It looks like magic. But, it is not!

Two things make a rainbow: water drops and sunlight.

Sunlight looks white, but it is made of different colors of light. When the Sun shines through water drops, the light breaks into different colors. That is why you cannot touch a rainbow. It is made of light!

You might see rainbows where there are water drops in the air. If the Sun shines through rain, you might see a rainbow. You might also see a rainbow near a waterfall or a fountain.

You always see the colors in a rainbow in the same order.

Red ➔ Orange ➔ Yellow ➔ Green ➔ Blue ➔ Purple

1. What two things are needed to make a rainbow?

_____

_____

2. Why can't you touch a rainbow?

_____

_____

3. Color the rainbow. Be sure to put the colors in rainbow order! Start with **red**.

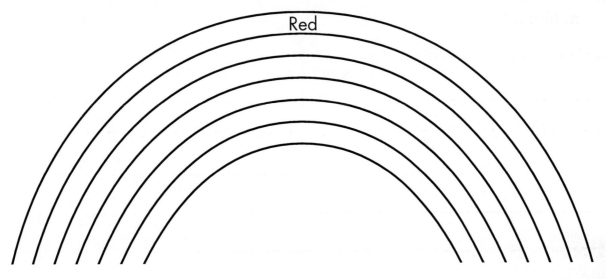

Red

Name: _____

Slow Changes to Earth: Part 1

Have you ever seen or touched sand? Do you know what it is made of? Sand is made of tiny pieces of rock. How do the rocks get so small? How does so much sand get on a beach? Land on Earth changes slowly through weathering, erosion, and deposition.

Break It

Weathering is when rocks break into smaller pieces. Weathering takes a long time. These are some ways that weathering can happen:

➤ Water moves rocks, so they rub against each other and break.

➤ Wind blows sand against rocks, and the rocks wear away.

➤ Plant roots grow between rocks and break them.

Take It

Erosion is when the small bits of rock are moved from one place to another. This can happen slowly or quickly. These are some ways that erosion can happen:

➤ Moving water carries bits of rock away.

➤ Wind blows bits of rock away.

➤ Gravity pulls bits of rock downhill.

Drop It

Deposition is when the small bits of rock are dropped in a new place. It can take a long time, or it can happen quickly. These are some ways that deposition can happen:

➤ Moving water drops bits of rock in a new place.

➤ Rocks roll down and settle at the bottom of a hill.

➤ Wind pushes sand around and makes sand dunes.

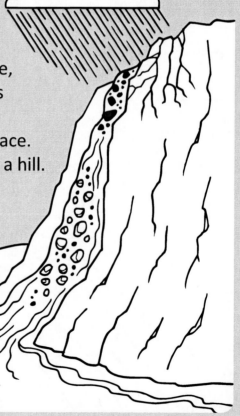

Name: _____

Slow Changes to Earth: Part 2

Directions: Write the definition of each term in the diagram.

Weathering

_____

_____

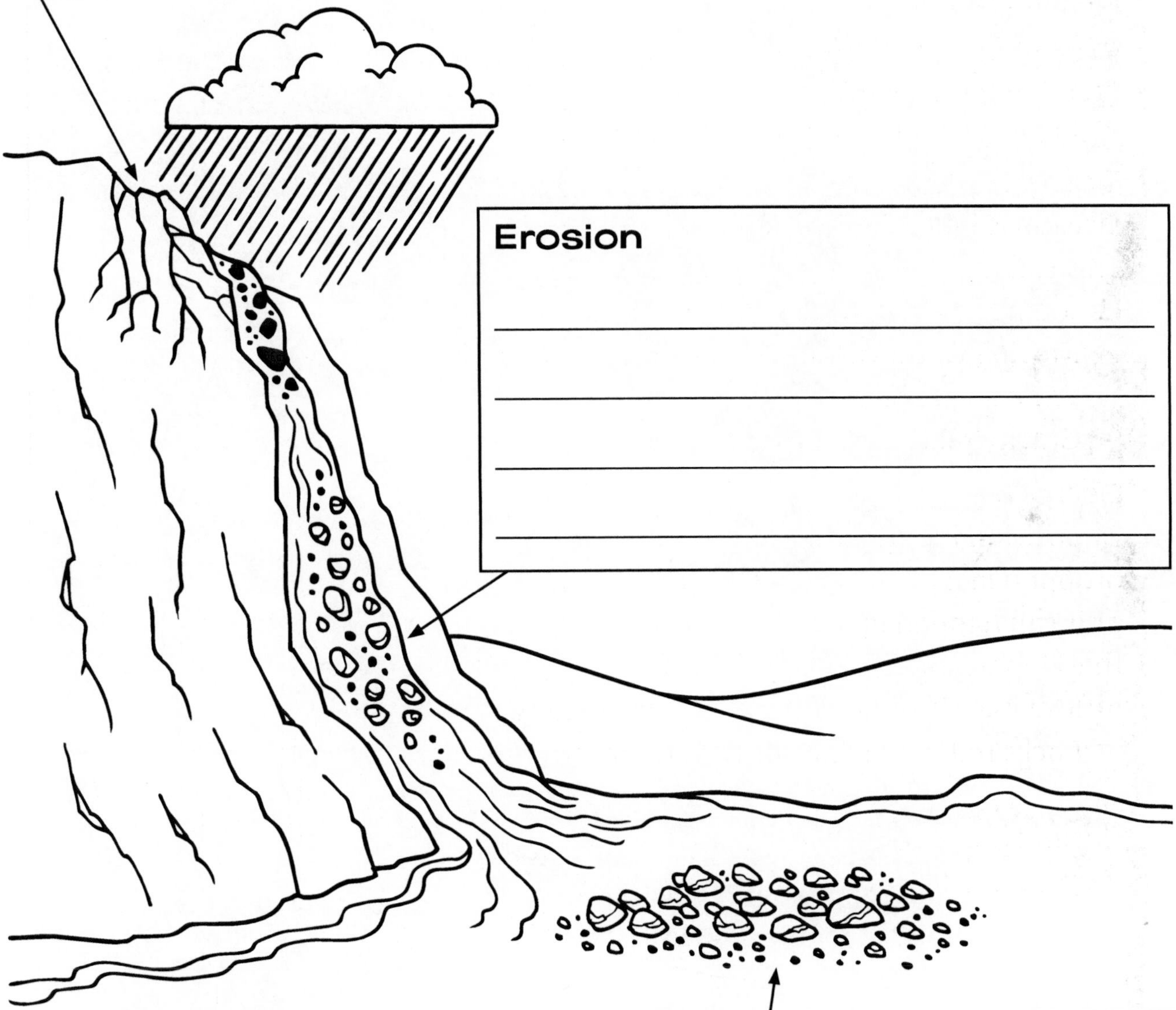

Erosion

_____

_____

_____

_____

Deposition

_____

_____

Name: _____

Volcanoes

Earth is not solid all the way through. It has hot, melted rock inside. The part we live on is called the **crust**. It floats on top of the melted rock. The crust is very thin. It is like the skin on an apple.

Melted rock is under the crust. It is called **magma**. Magma can come up between cracks in the crust. It spurts out or oozes out, forming a **volcano**. The melted rock that comes out is called **lava**.

Not all volcanoes are the same. Some are really tall. They blow a lot of lava and ash into the air. Others are like big bowls. The lava flows over the edges. Sometimes, lava makes a huge bubble and then pops!

Volcanoes change the land very quickly. When lava comes out of a volcano, it is gooey. It flows like water. Lava hardens when it cools. This makes new rocks and buries land.

Volcanoes can even make new islands when they erupt. Volcanoes made all the islands in Hawaii. One of the islands still has volcanic eruptions today!

Volcanoes don't erupt all the time. Some erupt every few years. Some go thousands of years between eruptions. All volcanoes go **dormant** (stop erupting) at some point. They may erupt again someday.

1. What is *magma*?
   a. an island
   b. melted rock coming out of a volcano
   c. melted rock under the ground

2. Volcanoes can change the land very _____.

3. How can volcanoes change the land? _____

_____

_____

Name: _____

Earthquakes

The land we live on feels solid. We think that it doesn't move. But it does!

Earth has hot, melted rock inside. It is not hard. It is gooey like pudding. The land we live on is called the **crust**. It floats on top of the melted rock inside Earth.

Earth's crust floats in big pieces called **plates**. The plates of Earth's crust fit together like puzzle pieces. Because they are floating, they move a little all the time. They bump and rub against each other.

Usually, we can't feel the plates moving. They only move about six inches in a year. Once in a while, two plates bump against each other very hard. Then, we feel an earthquake. During an earthquake, the movement travels through the ground like a wave. We feel the ground shake and roll.

Small earthquakes don't do much damage. But, a big earthquake can change things in a hurry! Cracks can appear in the ground. Moving land and falling rocks might make a stream change its course. Roads break and crack. Buildings can break or fall down.

1. Earth's *crust* floats in big pieces called _____.
   a. plates
   b. pudding
   c. earthquakes

2. We live on Earth's _____. It floats on top of hot, melted

   _____.

3. How can earthquakes change the land? _____

   _____

   _____

Name: _____

Water Changes the Land

When you drink a glass of water, you might not think about how strong water can be. But water can change the land!

Moving water can *slowly* make big changes in the land. It can take a very long time.

➡ Waves can wear away rocks near the ocean.

➡ A **glacier** is a river of ice that moves very slowly. The ice can even pick up very big rocks and move them.

➡ A river can carve a deep canyon.

A lot of water all at once can change the land *quickly*.

➡ A storm can bring a lot of rain. The rain can wash away dirt and bits of rock. Storms can make big changes to the land.

➡ A flood is when a lot of water spreads across the land. Floods can change the land quickly by washing away a lot of dirt. They can change the way streams and rivers flow.

➡ An earthquake can cause a giant wave called a **tsunami**. A tsunami is very powerful. The water rushes up onto the land. It pulls rocks, dirt, trees, and many other things back into the ocean.

1. What are two ways water can change the land slowly?

_____

_____

2. What are two ways water can change the land quickly?

_____

_____

3. What is the difference between a *glacier* and a *tsunami*?

_____

_____

Name: _____

Quick or Slow Change?

Directions: Write each word in the correct part of the Venn diagram.

Word Bank	deposition	tsunami	volcano	weathering
	glacier	earthquake	erosion	flood

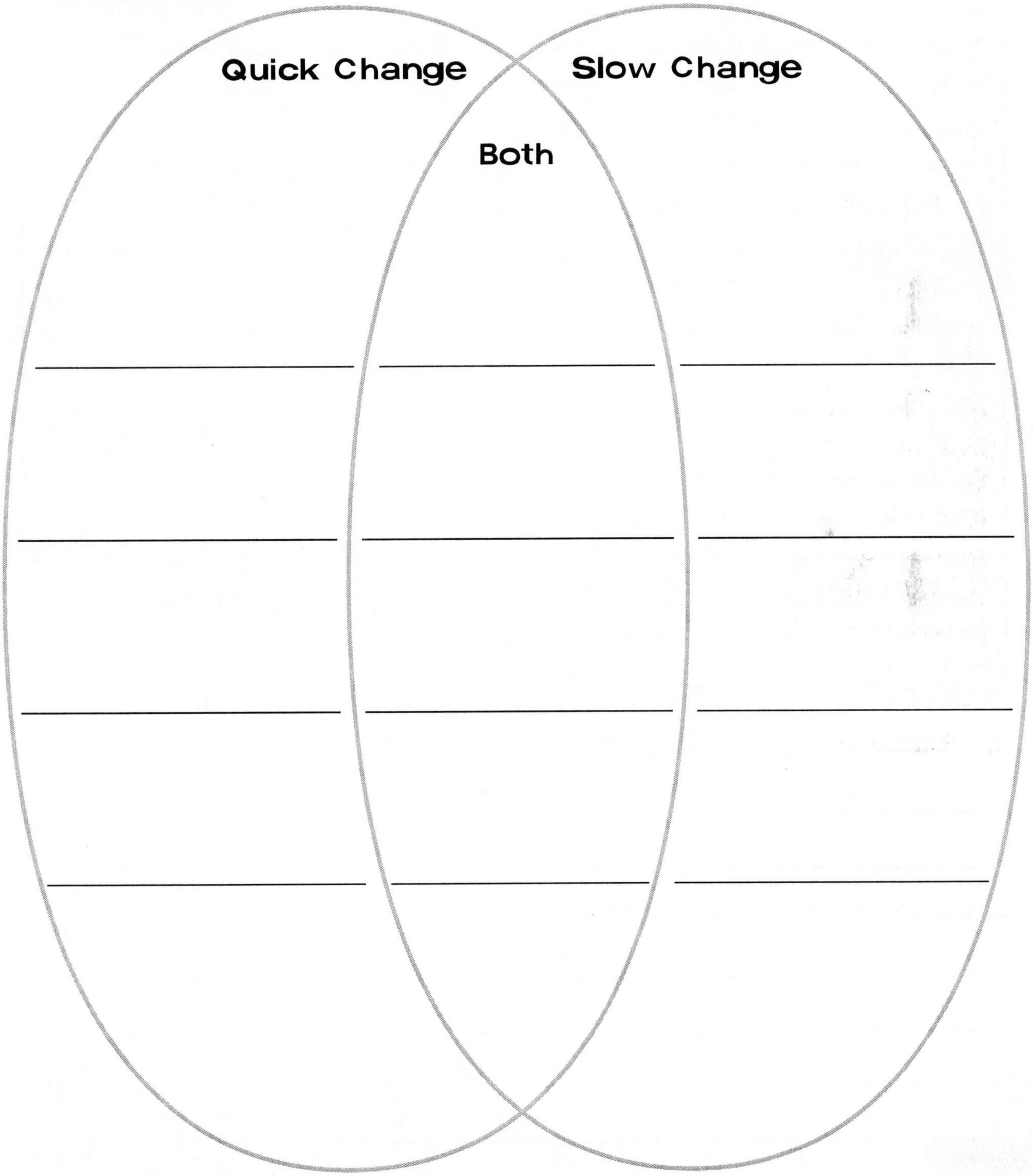

Quick Change   **Slow Change**

Both

Name: _____

The Water Cycle

Have you ever seen a lake or an ocean? It looks like a lot of water. Where does all that water come from? Water on Earth does not stay in the same place. It moves through the **water cycle**. The water cycle goes around and around. It never stops. It has no beginning and no end. Water is always moving on Earth.

➡ **Evaporation:** The Sun warms the water at the top of lakes and oceans. Tiny bits of water turn into water vapor. The water vapor goes up into the air. It is a gas. You cannot see it.

➡ **Condensation:** As the water vapor gets higher in the air, it cools off. The water turns into tiny drops. The water drops make clouds.

➡ **Precipitation:** The water drops get bigger and heavier. They fall from the clouds as rain or snow.

➡ **Collection:** The water flows back to the lakes and oceans.

Directions: Label the *water cycle*. Write the correct word in each box.

Word Bank

condensation

evaporation

collection

precipitation

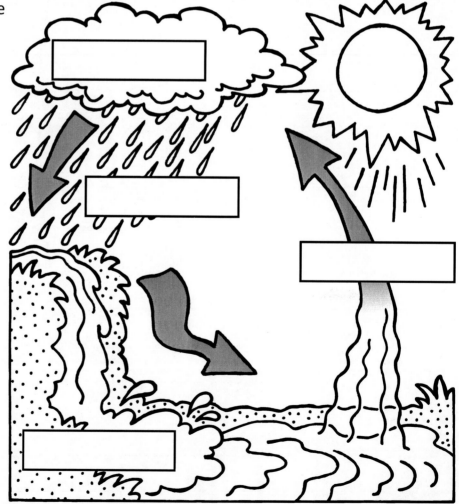

Name: _____

Where Is the Water on Earth?

Did you know Earth is sometimes called the "blue planet"? This is because water covers most of Earth.

Water is the reason there are living things on Earth. All living things need water to live. Plants need water. Animals need water. People need water!

➡ We must drink water to stay alive.

➡ We use it for cooking and cleaning.

➡ We use water to grow plants for food.

Almost all the water on Earth is **salt water** in oceans. It is too salty for us to drink or use for cooking. It is too salty to water plants. We cannot use most of the water on Earth.

Only a very small part of the water on Earth is fresh water. We can't use most of it because it is frozen. Some is frozen in big sheets of ice called **glaciers**. Some water is frozen in the **ice caps** that cover the top and bottom of Earth.

So, how do we get water we can use? Some fresh water is under the ground in **aquifers**. Water soaks into the ground. It collects in tiny holes and cracks in rocks. An aquifer is like a big sponge under the ground. People dig wells down into aquifers to get fresh water.

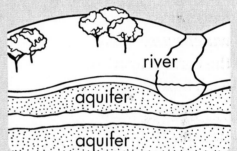

Only a tiny bit of the fresh water on Earth makes lakes, streams, rivers, and ponds. We can use this water. But we have to be careful not to use it all up!

1. What is an *aquifer*?

   a. water under the ground

   b. water in the ocean

   c. water in lakes and rivers

2. Why can't we use most of the water on Earth? _____

_____

3. How do you use water? Can you name three different ways?

_____

_____

Name: _____

Salt Water

Have you ever been swimming in an ocean? When you got water in your mouth, what did you taste? Salt!

The water in the ocean is salt water. Salt in the ocean comes from rocks on land. Rain falls on the rocks. It wears away the rocks a tiny bit at a time. The salty minerals in the rocks go into the water. The water flows down streams and rivers to the ocean. Over a very long time, more and more salt gets into the ocean waters.

Some lakes have salty water, too. They fill up with fresh water from rain and snow. Some of the water evaporates. It leaves the salt and minerals behind. The Great Salt Lake gets its name from its very salty water.

Most of the water on Earth is salt water. Humans cannot use salt water to live. It is not good to drink a lot of salt water. We cannot use it for cooking or cleaning. But oceans are important. Many animals live in salt water. Without oceans, there would be no sea turtles or whales!

1. It is not good for you to drink a lot of _____.
    a. fresh water   **b.** salt water

2. Rain washes _____ from rocks into rivers.

   The rivers take the salt to the _____.

3. Why are oceans important?

   _____

   _____

   _____

Name: _____

Ice on Earth

When water gets cold enough, it turns into ice. Most of the fresh water on Earth is frozen. Some of the ice forms in oceans, but when salt water freezes, the salt does not freeze with it. So, all the ice on Earth is made of fresh water.

➡ **Glaciers** are large rivers of ice. A glacier is formed when snow falls and does not melt. More snow falls on top of it. Layers of snow build up until they are very heavy. The weight of the snow pushes down and turns into ice. Glaciers move very, very slowly.

➡ **Polar ice caps** are huge sheets of ice. They form where the weather is cold all year long. If you look at a picture of Earth, you will see the ice caps. They are the white areas at the North and South Pole. The ice cap at the South Pole is so big it covers a whole continent—Antarctica!

➡ **Sea ice** is ice that floats on the ocean. At the North Pole, sea ice covers the entire ocean in winter. In summer, it gets smaller as some of it melts. Sometimes, huge chunks of ice break off and float away. These are called **icebergs**.

Directions: Write the correct word under each photo.

Word Bank	glacier	iceberg	sea ice

1. _____ 2. _____ 3. _____

Name: _____

Keep Water Clean

If you go to the sink for water, clean, fresh water should come out. But, where does clean water come from?

In many places, the water is pumped up from under the ground. In other places, the water comes from lakes or rivers. Water must be cleaned before it goes through pipes to our homes and schools.

Where does the dirty water go when you brush your teeth, take a shower, or flush a toilet? It goes to a place where it is cleaned. Some of it is used to water plants and grass. Some of it is put back under the ground or into lakes and rivers. It goes back into the water cycle.

Some things are hard to clean out of water. We should never put bad things like bug spray, paint, or oil into the water. Living things need clean, fresh water to live. We must make sure that we keep our water clean.

We must take care of the oceans, too. Half of the kinds of animals and plants on Earth live in the oceans. And, there are many more that we don't know about yet! We need to keep the oceans clean for the plants and animals that live there.

1. Which of these is true?
   a. Water is cleaned using bleach and oil.
   b. Fresh water does not need to be cleaned.
   c. Water is cleaned *before* it goes to your house and *after* it leaves your house.

2. What are three places that our water can come from?

   _____   _____   _____

3. Why should we keep lakes, rivers, and oceans clean?

   _____

   _____

   _____

Name: _____

Landforms

The land on Earth is not the same all over. It is made of different **landforms**. Landforms are the different shapes of land on Earth. Some landforms are low, like valleys. Some are high, like mountains.

Some landforms go together.
- ➡ Low landforms are next to tall landforms.
- ➡ Valleys form in between hills.
- ➡ Mountains rise from flat plains.

Landforms do not stay the same. They are always changing. Wind and water break rocks into smaller pieces. The small pieces get moved to new places.

Landforms can change slowly.
- ➡ A mountain can wear away to become a hill over millions of years.
- ➡ A river can cut a canyon deep into the land.

Quick changes can happen, too.
- ➡ A volcano can make a new island or mountain.
- ➡ Earthquakes can cause cracks in Earth. They can push mountains a bit higher.

1. *Landforms* are _____.
   a. small pieces of rock
   b. large earthquakes
   c. different shapes of land

2. *Landforms* do not stay the _____. They are always

   _____.

3. How can *landforms* change slowly?

   _____

   _____

   _____

Name: _____

Mountains and Hills

Mountains are the tallest landforms on Earth. They rise high above the land around them. They have rocky tops that can be rounded or pointy. The top of a mountain is called the **peak**. It can be very cold at the peak of a mountain. Trees don't grow there. Some mountains have snow and ice at the top all year long.

Mountain

Where do mountains come from? Some are formed when two plates of Earth's crust push into each other. The edges of the plates push up. This makes a group of mountains called a **range**. This happens very slowly. It takes millions of years for these mountain ranges to form. The Himalayan mountains were formed this way. This mountain range includes Mount Everest. It reaches higher toward the sky than any other mountain.

Others mountains are made by volcanoes. Mauna Kea is the tallest mountain made by a volcano. Its base is under the ocean. Its top sticks out of the ocean and helps form the island of Hawaii. It is taller than Everest when measured from the bottom to the top.

Hills

A **hill** is also higher than the land around it. It has sloping sides. Hills are not as steep or as high as mountains. It is sometimes hard to tell the difference between a hill and a mountain. Even scientists can't agree!

1. The top of a mountain is called the _____.
   a. peak   **b.** range   **c.** hill

2. A group of mountains is called a _____.

3. Describe one way that mountains are formed. _____

_____

_____

Name: _____

Valleys and Canyons

Mountains rise up above the land around them. The low area between mountains is called a **valley**. Rain and melting snow run down the sides of the mountain. They can make a river at the bottom of the valley. The river carries away bits of rock and dirt from the land. This gives a valley its **V** shape.

Valley

Glen Canyon

A **canyon** is a narrow, deep valley. It has steep cliffs on each side. The most famous canyon is the Grand Canyon. It took millions of years for the river to slowly dig its way through the rock.

Glaciers can change the shape of valleys. Glaciers are very slow-moving rivers of ice. The ice picks up rocks and drags them along the valley floor. It grinds away some of the land. The **V** shape turns into a **U** shape.

1. A *valley* is _____.
   a. rain and melting snow
   b. a river of ice
   c. a low area between mountains or hills

2. A _____ is a narrow, deep valley with steep cliffs on each side.

3. Why are some valleys U-shaped?

   _____

   _____

   _____

Name: _____

Plains

Plains are large, flat areas of land. Plains cover more than one third of Earth. There are plains on every continent.

Flood plains are formed by rivers. The water in a river sometimes overflows. It spreads out along the land. There is lots of mud and sand in the water. It stays behind as the waters go back. This happens again and again over many years, and the soil builds up. Flood plains are good for growing plants.

Plains

Grasslands are plains where grass grows. The grass can be very tall if the soil is good and there is enough rain. Where it is hot and dry, the grasses are shorter.

In the coldest places, plains are called tundras. The ground is frozen most of the year. It is very windy. The plants are very small and low to the ground. This helps them stay warm.

Lava field

Lava fields are formed when lots of lava from a volcano flows across a flat area. At first, plants cannot grow on the cooled lava rock. Over time, wind and rain break down the rock. Soil forms. Lava fields can become grasslands.

1. A *plain* is _____.
   a. a low place between mountains
   b. frozen ground
   c. a large, flat area of land

2. *Flood plains* are formed by _____.

3. Describe how a *lava field* can turn into a grassland.

   _____

   _____

   _____

Name: _____

People Change the Land

People have always changed the land. A long time ago, people cut down trees to make farms and houses. They dug in the ground to find water. Most of the changes they made were small because they only had hand tools. It took a lot of work to make big changes.

Now, we have big machines. We can dig bigger holes and cut down more trees in a shorter time. There are more and more people on Earth all the time. We change the land for many reasons.

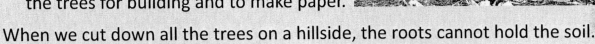

- We cut down trees to clear land for farming. We need more land for more farms to grow more food.
- We also cut trees to get wood. We use the trees for building and to make paper.

When we cut down all the trees on a hillside, the roots cannot hold the soil. When it rains, there is a lot of **erosion**. This can cause floods and other problems.

- We cut into the land to build roads. We dig tunnels through mountains.
- We drill deep into Earth for oil. We dig away parts of the land to find coal and natural gas. We use these to power factories, homes, and cars.
- We dig into hills and mountains to find copper and other minerals.

1. What are two reasons people cut down trees?

   Reason 1: _____

   Reason 2: _____

2. What are two reasons people change the land?

   Reason 1: _____

   Reason 2: _____

3. When too many trees are cut down at once, it can cause _____.

Name: _____

Water on Earth

Water covers most of Earth. When you look at a picture of Earth taken from space, you see that most of it is blue. All that blue is water. That is why some people call Earth the "big, blue marble."

Remember the water cycle? It moves water all over Earth. What happens to water that falls from clouds onto the ground?

Water runs from higher ground to lower ground. The water flows in **streams** and **rivers**. These take water from one place to another. The water collects in oceans and lakes.

Oceans are the biggest bodies of water. They hold most of the water on Earth. There are five oceans. They are all connected.

Lakes are big bodies of water. There are many lakes in the world. Some lakes are very big, and some are small. Lakes can get deeper as more water flows into them. They get shallower when more water flows out.

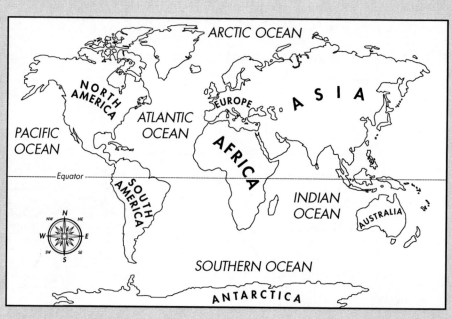

1. _____ are the biggest bodies of water on Earth.
   a. Lakes   **b.** Oceans   **c.** Rivers

2. Water falls from clouds and flows from higher to lower ground. This creates rivers

   and _____. It collects in oceans and _____.

3. Why do some people call Earth the "big, blue marble"?

   _____

   _____

Name: _____

Oceans

Earth has five oceans. They are the biggest bodies of water on Earth. Oceans are so big that it takes ships many days to cross them.

Oceans are salt water. Salt in ocean water comes from rocks on land. Rainwater carries the salt down rivers to the ocean. We cannot drink the salty ocean water.

Some parts of the oceans are miles deep. The deep parts of the ocean are always cold. Some parts near land are very shallow. The Sun warms the water at the top of the ocean.

The **surface** water near the middle of Earth gets warm. Those areas get more sunlight. The surface water near the top and bottom of Earth is very cold. It is so cold that much of it is covered in ice!

It's **cold** up here!

Ahh... nice and warm here in the middle.

It's even **colder** down here!

The land around an ocean is called the **coast**. An ocean's coast might have tall cliffs or shallow, sandy beaches. A **gulf** is a large area of an ocean that has land on three sides.

1. How many oceans are on Earth?
   a. 3   **b.** 4   **c.** 5

2. The Sun warms the _____ of the oceans.

3. Why is the water in the ocean salty?

   _____

   _____

   _____

Name: _____

Rivers and Streams

Have you ever spilled a cup of water? What happens? If you spill it onto the floor, the water spreads out and stops moving. This is like a lake. If you spill it onto your lap, it runs down your legs onto the floor. This is like a river. Rivers are different from lakes because the water in a river is always moving downhill.

A river starts when rain and melting snow run down the sides of a hill or a mountain. The start of a river is called its **source**. Small streams flow together to make a river. The water moves from land that is higher to land that is lower.

Some rivers flow into a lake. The water stays in the lake for a while. Then, the river starts up again on the downhill end of the lake. More and more water enters a river as it flows. It gets bigger and bigger. The water keeps moving until it reaches an ocean. The end of a river is called the **mouth**.

Rivers can make big changes in the land. Where they move fast, they can wear away dirt and rock to make canyons. They can drop lots of dirt and rock where they slow down.

1. The start of a river is called its _____.
   a. source
   b. mouth
   c. flow

2. Water in a river is always moving _____.

3. How can rivers make changes in the land?

   _____

   _____

Name: _____

Lakes

A lake is a large body of water with land around it. The water in a lake does not flow like a river. It mostly stays still. Some lakes are very big. You cannot see from one side to the other. Some lakes are very small. How many lakes are there on Earth? Too many to count!

Most lakes have fresh water. Water from rain and melting snow runs downhill in a stream or a river. The river flows into the uphill side of a lake. There is usually a river at the lower end of a fresh water lake, too. These lakes are called **open** lakes. Water slowly goes out of the lake into the river. It flows toward the ocean.

Open lake

Closed lake

Some lakes have salty water. These lakes do not have a river at the lower end. These are called **closed** lakes. The water stays in the lake and **evaporates**. It leaves a lot of salt behind.

People can make lakes. They build a **dam**, like a wall, across a river. It stops the water from flowing. The water gets deeper as the lake fills up behind the dam. We can use the fresh water for farms and cities.

Dam

1. A large body of water with land all around it is a _____.

   a. lake   **b.** river   **c.** dam

2. People can make a lake by building a _____ across a river.

3. Why do some lakes have salty water?

_____

_____

Name: _____

People Change Water on Earth

All living things need clean, fresh water. People use water every day. We drink water. We cook and clean with water. Sometimes, the ways we get fresh water can change bodies of water on Earth.

- We take fresh water from rivers and lakes. We send it to cities and farms for people to use. The rivers can get smaller or go dry before they reach a lake or an ocean. Lakes can get smaller or disappear.

- People build dams on rivers. A new lake forms behind the dam. What used to be land is now under water. The river stops flowing below the dam. Places that had a lot of water are now drier.

- People fill in shallow water at the edge of a lake or an ocean with dirt. They build cities on top. Sometimes, they dig at the bottom of the lake or ocean to make it even deeper. They build docks for big ships.

Sometimes, we make lake or ocean water dirty. We put trash and chemicals in the water. We say the water is **polluted**. This makes the water bad for living things. We need to keep the water on Earth clean!

1. What kind of water do people need to live?
    a. salt water   **b.** polluted water   **c.** clean, fresh water

2. When people build a _____, a new lake is formed.

3. Why do we take fresh water from rivers and lakes?

_____

_____

Name: _____

What Is a Map?

What is a map? A map is a drawing that tells you about a place.

How do we use maps?

- People use maps to find out about a place.
- A map can help people find out how to get somewhere.
- Scientists use maps to learn about landforms and bodies of water.

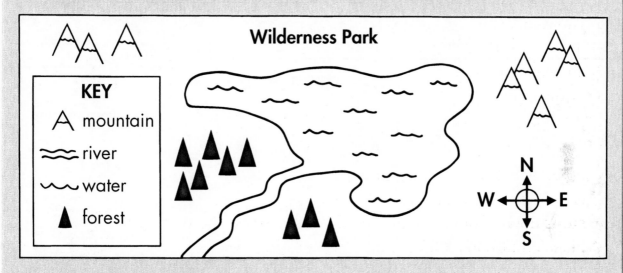

What are the main parts of a map?

- The **title** of the map tells what area is shown on the map.
- The **compass rose** shows which direction to go to find things on the map.
- The **symbols** show where things such as forests and rivers are on the map.
- The **map key** shows what each symbol on the map means.
- **Land** shown on a map is usually green or brown. **Water** on a map is blue.

1. Color the land on the map above green or brown. Color the water blue.

2. What is the title of the map? _____

3. Where can you look to find out what this symbol 〰 means? _____

_____

4. What does this symbol ⋀ mean? _____

5. What part of the map shows you which way north is? _____

Name: _____

Map Keys and Symbols

Symbols are small lines or shapes on a map. They help make reading a map easier. Each symbol stands for a different feature. Symbols might be lines or patterns. They might be little pictures. If you see a little mountain on a map, that probably means there is a mountain in that place!

Sometimes, it is hard to tell what the symbols mean. If you don't understand what a symbol on a map is, look for a **map key**. A map key tells you what each symbol stands for.

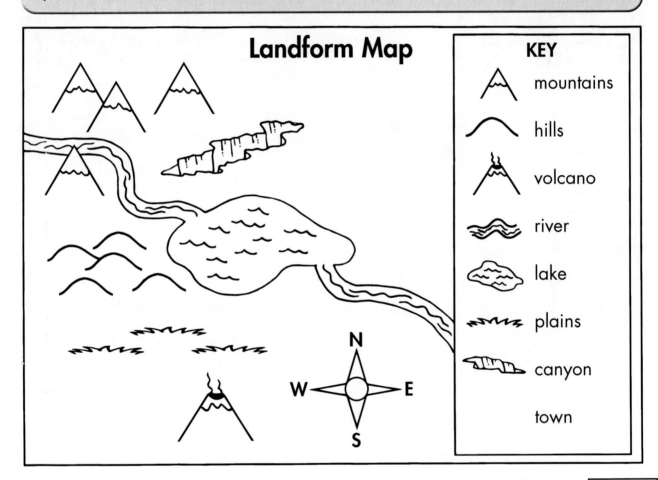

1. What does this symbol ~~~ mean? _____.

2. What is on the map that runs between the mountains? Draw its symbol.

3. How many volcanoes are on the map? _____ Draw the volcano symbol.

4. Draw some more mountains east of the canyon.

5. Create a symbol for a town. Add it to the map key next to the word *town*.

6. Think about where a good place for a town would be. Draw it on the map.

Name: _____

Compass Rose

A **compass rose** is a symbol on a map. It shows which way north, south, east, and west are on the map. These directions help us find things on a map. Most maps are drawn with north at the top.

Most people can remember that north is at the top of the compass rose and south is at the bottom. But, it can be hard to remember which way is east and which way is west. Here is a little trick: If you put **W** and **E** on the compass rose in the right places, they spell the word *we*!

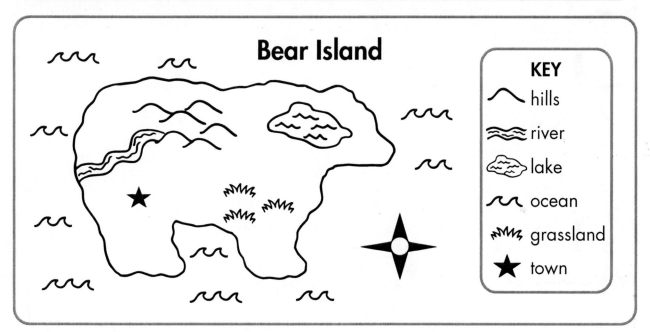

1. Label **N**, **S**, **E**, and **W** on the compass rose.

2. The lake is _____ of the hills.

3. The town is _____ of the river.

4. Which direction will you go from the town to the grassland?   **N   S   E   W**

5. Write directions for going from the town to the lake.

_____

_____

Name: _____

What Is a Globe?

Maps are flat. They are good for showing people how to get from place to place. Most maps show a part of Earth.

Earth is round like a ball, not flat like a map. **Globes** are round so they can show the whole Earth. You can turn a globe around and look at all the continents and the oceans. Some globes also show the outlines of countries.

A globe often has a compass rose. It is easy to tell north and south on a globe. North is up and south is down. The point at the very top of the globe is the North Pole, and the point at the very bottom is the South Pole.

The equator is a line that goes around the middle of the globe. It is not really a line on Earth. It is only on a globe. It is halfway between the North Pole and the South Pole.

Directions

1. Color the land green.

2. Color the water blue.

3. Draw a red line for the equator.

4. Draw an arrow and an **S** to show the South Pole. Label it.

5. Draw an arrow and an **N** to show the North Pole. Label it.

Name: _____

Comparing Maps and Globes

Some things about globes and maps are the same. They are both pictures that give us information about places. They both help us find places.

Maps and globes are also different from each other. A map is easy to carry with you. You can fold it and put it in a bag or a pocket. You might have a map on a phone.

A globe would be hard to carry with you. A globe shows all of Earth, but maps sometimes only show one part of Earth. Maps can show more details than globes. A map usually has a map key, but a globe does not.

Directions: Write each item in the correct place in the Venn diagram.

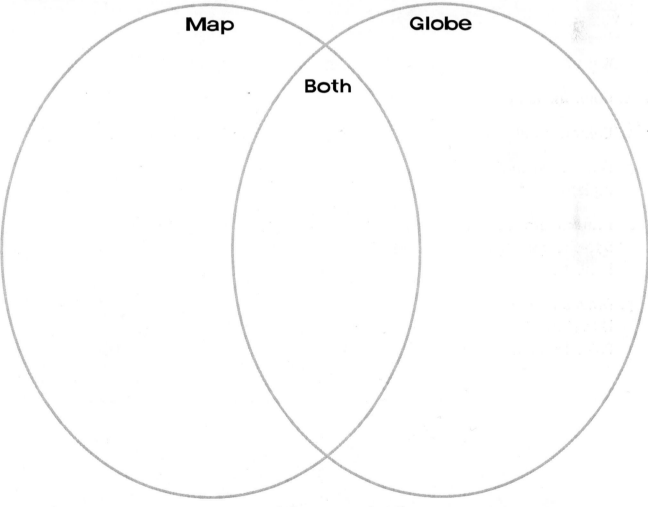

- flat
- round
- may only show small areas
- shows the whole planet

- shows more details
- shows fewer details
- helps us find places
- has a map key

- easy to carry
- hard to carry
- gives us information about a place

Name: _____

What Are Properties of Materials?

The things around you are made of **materials**. Pencils are made of wood. Scissors are made of metal. Cups can be made of glass or plastic.

- We can **observe** things and the materials they are made from. We look at them and feel them. Some things we can smell and taste.

- We can **describe** materials and objects. *Describe* means to talk about what something is like. To describe a pencil, you might say it is long, thin, and hard. You might say it has a point at one end. You can use your senses to observe and describe the materials. You can see that your pencil is long and thin. You can feel that it is hard.

We can use the **properties** of materials to put things into groups. Your desk, your chair, and the floor are hard. Your clothes, your hair, and a cotton ball are soft.

1. How would you make two groups with these items? Circle your groups.

marble

orange

box

ball

sandwich

cracker

2. Think about their properties. Write a label for each box on the top line.

3. Write the names of the items under the correct label.

Name: _____

Describing Properties of Materials

You describe properties of matter all the time. You might say, "I want to wear my blue shirt today." You are describing the color of the shirt. Or you could say, "This hot chocolate is too hot." You are describing how the food feels.

We can use special words to describe an object's properties.

- A towel is *soft*, and a rock is *hard*.
- Metal is *shiny*, and wood is *dull*.
- An eraser is *flexible*. This means it can bend.
- A pencil is *hard*. It cannot bend without breaking.

1. Choose an object in the classroom. Don't say what it is!

   Describe its **size**. _____

   Describe its **shape**. _____

   Describe its **color**. _____

   Describe **what it feels like**. _____

   How else would you describe its properties? _____

   _____

   _____

2. Trade papers with a partner. Read the description your partner wrote. What object do you think your partner was describing?

   _____

3. Could your partner tell what object you described?   **Yes**   **No**

Name: _____

Observing with the Senses

We can use our senses to find out about the properties of materials.

1 We can **see** color, shape, and size. Describe what you see when you look at a tree. _____ _____	
2 We can **feel** if things are hot, bumpy, or bendy. Describe what you feel when you touch a rubber band. _____ _____	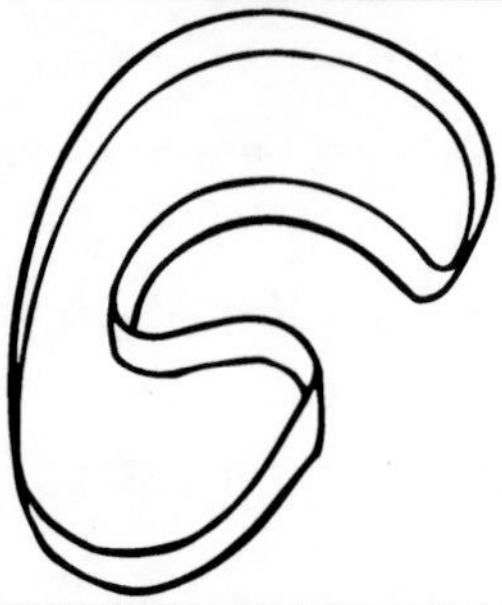
3 We can **hear** how loud or high-pitched a sound is. What does a lion's roar sound like? _____ _____	
4 We can **taste** sour, sweet, salty, and bitter. What is your favorite food? _____ What does your favorite food taste like? _____ Draw your favorite food in the box. ⟶	**my favorite food** ↘
5 We can **smell** how strong a smell is and if it is nice or yucky. What does an orange smell like? _____ _____	

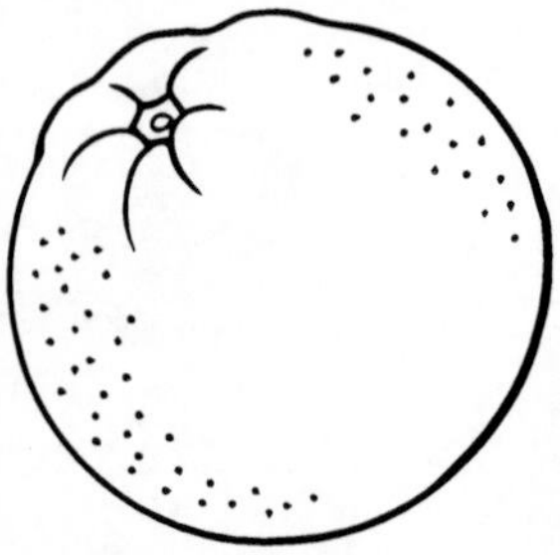

Name: _____

Uses of Materials

Would you use plastic cups or rubber bands to build a tower? You would use cups because they are **rigid.** They do not squish or bend easily. Rubber bands are too **flexible.** They would not to stay up.

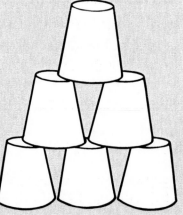

We use materials to make things. We choose the materials that will do the best job. We make buildings out of wood and metal. Those materials are rigid and strong. You would not want to build a house out of cotton or jelly!

We make windows out of glass so you can see through them. Metal and wood do not make very good windows.

1. If you wanted to make a nest for a baby bird, what materials would you use?

_____

Why? _____

2. Pretend you want to build a bridge from your table to your friend's table. Circle the materials you would use to build a bridge.

dry noodles

craft sticks

marbles

cotton balls

books

pencils

tissues

3. Why did you choose these materials for your bridge? _____

_____

4. Draw your idea for a bridge.

Name: _____

Changing Properties of Materials

Sometimes, we can change the properties of materials. This can help us use them in new ways.

Wood from a tree can be rough. If you touch it, you might get a splinter. We can cut the wood. We can smooth it with tools. Then, we can use it to make a chair or a table.

We can stretch a rubber band to make it longer. This helps it go around things and hold them together.

Clay is a material we can change in many ways. We can squish it. We can roll it flat. We can pinch it into a pot.

Directions: Describe how you could change the properties of each material.

1. clay

_____

_____

2. aluminum foil

_____

_____

3. string

_____

_____

Name: _____

Matter

Everything around you is made of **matter**. Anything that takes up space is matter. Water is made of matter. The air you breathe is made of matter. You are made of matter!

On Earth, most matter is in one of three **states**: solid, liquid, or gas. Each state is made up of small pieces of matter. These small pieces of matter are called **particles**. These particles act differently in each state.

Solids keep their shape. Your desk is solid. The walls of your room are solid.

➡ In a solid, the particles stay locked close together. They hold their shape.

Liquids do not have their own shape. They spread out and take the shape of their container. If you pour water into a cup, it takes the shape of the cup. If you pour a liquid into a bowl, it will take the shape of the bowl.

➡ The particles in a liquid are connected loosely. They slide past each other easily. So, a liquid flows and pours.

Gases do not have a shape. They fill up their containers. If you put air into a balloon, the balloon gets bigger. The air does not sit at the bottom of the balloon. It fills the balloon.

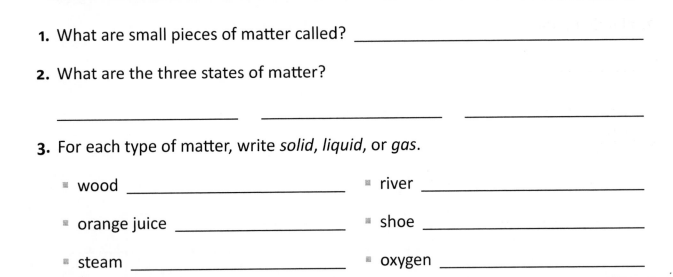

➡ The particles in a gas are not connected. They are constantly moving, and they move very fast! They are much more spread out than liquids or solids.

1. What are small pieces of matter called? _____

2. What are the three states of matter?

   _____ _____ _____

3. For each type of matter, write *solid*, *liquid*, or *gas*.

   ▪ wood _____   ▪ river _____

   ▪ orange juice _____   ▪ shoe _____

   ▪ steam _____   ▪ oxygen _____

Name: _____

Solids

Touch your desk. What do you feel? The matter in your desk is **solid**. Solids can be hard like your desk or soft like your hair. They can be big like a mountain or small like a grain of sand.

In a solid, the **particles** stay locked close together. They hold their shape unless something pushes or pulls on them. Even when you break a solid into pieces, each piece is still a solid. You can break a rock, but you can't pour it!

Some solids can fool you.

Do you think your shirt is a solid? It moves when you wear it. It can bend and fold. But the basic shape of the shirt stays the same. The particles are attached to each other and don't come apart. It is a solid.

Salt

Do you think salt is a solid? It is! Salt is made of small pieces. Each piece is solid. So even though you can pour salt, it is not a liquid.

Other solids made of small pieces are sugar, flour, and sand.

There are solids in your body. Your bones are solid. So are your teeth.

1. In a solid, the _____ stay locked together.

2. Which two are solids? Circle your answers.

                sugar   **milk**   **sand**   **juice**

3. What are three solids in or on your body?

_____

_____

_____

Name: _____

Liquids

Have you ever spilled a glass of water? What happens? It spreads out along the ground. Would the same thing happen if you dropped a solid such as an apple? No. It would keep its shape.

Liquids have no shape. They spread out and take the shape of their container. In a liquid, the particles stay close together, but not in the same position. They can slip and slide around. This means that liquids can flow and pour.

Imagine water coming out of a hose and going into a bucket. It flows out of the hose in a stream of water. It takes the shape of the bucket. Whatever container you put a liquid in, it will take that shape. The shape of a liquid can change, even when the volume or amount of liquid doesn't change.

Honey

Liquids can be thick or thin. A thin liquid flows easily. Water, juice, and milk are thin liquids. Thicker liquids flow more slowly. Pudding, oil, and honey are thick liquids.

There are liquids in your body. Blood is a liquid. So is sweat.

1. Which is true of a liquid?
   a. It spreads out and takes the shape of its container.
   b. The particles are locked together.
   c. Its shape doesn't change.

2. Name a thick liquid and a thin liquid.

   Thick liquid: _____

   Thin liquid: _____

3. Why can a liquid flow and pour?

   _____

   _____

Name: _____

Gases

Take a breath. What do you feel? Air is going into your lungs. Air is a **gas**. It is always all around us. You usually cannot see gases. You can feel them. When you feel the wind blowing, that is air moving.

Gases do not have a shape. They fill up their containers. If you put a gas into a balloon, the balloon gets bigger. The air does not sit at the bottom of the balloon. It expands to fill the whole space. No matter how big the balloon is or what shape it is, the gas will spread out and fill it up.

The particles in a gas are not connected to each other. They spread out and move around a lot. A gas will spread out evenly in any container, no matter how big. If a gas is let out of a container, it will spread out and become part of the air. If you open a can or bottle of soda, you will hear a *sssss* sound. That is a gas coming out of the container.

There are gases in your body. You breathe air in and out of your lungs all the time. Sometimes, you get extra air in your lungs or stomach. That gas is what comes out when you burp!

1. Which is not true of a *gas*?
    a. It does not have a shape.
    b. Its particles are not connected to each other.
    c. It is easy to see it.

2. Circle the three gases.

air	water	steam	oxygen	sound

3. Why do you burp?

_____

_____

Name: _____

Changing States of Matter

There are three states of matter—**solid**, **liquid**, and **gas**. Matter changes states when it gets hotter or colder. The **particles** in matter change how they are connected and how they move.

Water is matter. Water in the freezer gets really cold. The particles slow down a lot. They stick together. The liquid water becomes solid ice.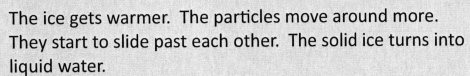

When a liquid turns into a solid, we say it **freezes**. What happens to an ice cube when you put it out in the sunlight?

The ice gets warmer. The particles move around more. They start to slide past each other. The solid ice turns into liquid water.

When a solid turns into a liquid, we say it **melts**. It loses its shape.

Have you ever watched a puddle on a hot day? It gets smaller until it is gone. What happens to the water?

When the water in the puddle gets hot, the particles start moving more. They move faster. The water turns into **water vapor**. When a liquid turns into a gas, we say it **evaporates**.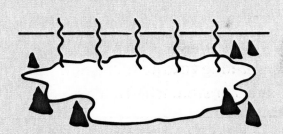

1. Frozen water is   **a solid**   **a liquid**   **a gas**.

2. When ice melts, it becomes   **a solid**   **a liquid**   **a gas**.

3. When water gets very, very hot, it starts to evaporate. It becomes a

   _____

4. What do the particles do when a liquid turns into a solid? _____

   _____

   _____

Name: _____

Two Kinds of Changes

Things change all the time. Night changes to day. You change from being asleep to being awake. Maybe you eat cereal for breakfast. The cereal changes when it goes from the bowl to your stomach! Which of these changes can be undone? Which cannot?

Sometimes, things can change back to the way they were. You change from asleep to awake. At night, the change is **reversed**. It goes back to the way it was. Day changes back to night, and you go back to sleep again.

Some changes can't go back. When you eat cereal, it goes into your body. Your body changes the cereal into energy. That change can't be reversed. You can't change the energy in your body back into cereal! If you break an egg and cook it, you cannot turn it back into a raw egg. If you toast a piece of bread, you cannot un-toast it.

Matter can change. Some changes to matter can be changed back. When ice gets warm, it melts. It changes into water. When water gets cold enough, it changes back into ice.

1. What does it mean when a change can be *reversed*?
    a. It can go back to the way it was.
    b. It cannot go back to the way it was.

2. Which of these is a change that cannot be reversed?
    a. You get hot from running fast.
    b. You grow two inches taller.
    c. You feel tired at bedtime.

3. Is blowing up a balloon a change that can be *reversed*?　　**Yes**　　**No**

    Explain: _____

    _____

Name: _____

Freezing and Melting

What happens if you leave ice cream out of the freezer for too long? It melts! When something **melts**, it turns from a solid to a liquid.

Some things will melt if they get just a little bit warm. Ice cream and ice pops melt into liquid if they are not in the freezer. Some things only melt if you make them warm or hot. Chocolate and candle wax will melt if you make them hot.

How do you make ice? You put water in the freezer. It changes to a solid. When something **freezes**, it turns from a liquid to a solid.

Some things become solid when you put them in the freezer. Water, juice, and ice cream need to be in the freezer to turn into solids. Some things become solid when they are in the refrigerator. Jell-O™ turns solid in the refrigerator.

What would happen if you put a pencil in the freezer? Would it change? No. A pencil doesn't change when you put it in the freezer. And it's okay to leave a pencil out in the Sun. It won't melt if it gets warm. Many solids, such as wood, paper, and metal, don't change when they get very, very cold. They don't melt when they get warm, either.

1. Which of these things will melt if you leave it out in the Sun?
   a. a spoon   **b.** an apple   **c.** an ice cube

2. Which of these will change to a liquid if it gets hot?
   a. a book   **b.** a crayon   **c.** paper

3. When you take ice cream out of the freezer, it is solid and hard. It is not easy to scoop it out of the container. How could you make the ice cream a little bit softer?
   a. Put it in the oven on high.
   b. Leave it on the counter for a little while.
   c. Put it back in the freezer.

4. If you leave a cup of chocolate candy out in the Sun, it will melt. Can this change be reversed?
   a. Yes, the chocolate can be made solid again.
   b. No, the chocolate cannot be made solid again.

Name: _____

Changes That Can't Be Reversed

Some changes can't be **reversed**. Once you make these kinds of changes, you can't get back the things you started with.

When something is cooked or burned, it can't go back to the way it was before.

➡ What happens when paper burns? It turns into smoke and ash. It can never be paper again.

➡ If you cook an egg, it changes. You can't turn it back into a raw egg.

➡ When something alive grows, it can't go back to the way it was before. You are always growing older. You can't go back to being younger.

➡ A baby chick grows into a chicken. It can never be a baby chick again.

➡ An apple seed grows into a tree. It can't go back to being a seed.

➡ When something dies or rots, it can't be alive again.

➡ When a banana gets old, it turns brown and mushy. It can't go back to being a yummy, yellow banana again.

➡ Leaves die and fall off a tree. They can't go back onto the tree and keep growing.

1. Burning paper is a change that can't be _____.
    a. helped
    b. liquid
    c. reversed

2. What is something that can be cooked and can't be changed back?

    _____

3. What is something that grows that can't be changed back?

    _____

Name: _____

Can It Change Back?

Directions: Read the stories. Answer the questions.

1   Dang's mom mixes eggs, flour, and sugar. She is making dough. She puts the dough on a tray. She bakes the cookies in the oven. Can the eggs be changed back?

            Yes   **No**

Explain: _____

2   Joy left her chocolate bar in her mom's car on a hot day. The chocolate melted. Can she make the chocolate solid again?

            Yes   **No**

Explain: _____

3   Mateo just had a birthday. He turned seven years old. Can he ever be six years old again?

            Yes   **No**

Explain: _____

4   Althea's dad poured juice into a paper cup. He put it in the freezer. He told her she could eat it like an ice pop. Althea doesn't want an ice pop. She wants to drink juice. Can she change the ice pop back into juice?

            Yes   **No**

Explain: _____

5   The Sun shines on a lake. Some of the water evaporates. It becomes water vapor. It goes up into the sky. It makes a cloud. Will the water vapor become water again?

            Yes   **No**

Explain: _____

Name: _____

Heat, Light, and Sound Energy

Energy is how things move and change. Energy cooks your food. Energy makes the Sun shine. You need energy to move and grow.

Heat, light, and sound are three kinds of energy:

- **Heat** is a kind of energy you can *feel*. Heat energy makes things warmer. Things get warmer when their particles move faster.

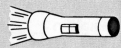

- **Light** is a kind of energy you can *see*. Light energy moves in a straight line. It can be natural or manmade.

- **Sound** is a kind of energy you can *hear*. Sound is made when particles **vibrate**. Vibrate means to move back and forth very quickly. We hear vibrations with our ears. Sound can travel through solids, liquids, and gases.

1. What are two things that energy can do?

_____

_____

2. You can _____ light energy.

3. You can _____ sound energy.

4. You can _____ heat energy.

5 Draw something that gets warmer.	**6** Draw something that makes light.	**7** Draw a sound you can hear.

Name: _____

Heat

Heat is energy you can feel. Heat energy makes things warmer. We use heat energy to cook our food. Heat energy keeps our bodies warm when it is cold.

All things are made of small bits called **particles**. Particles are so small that you can't see them. They are always moving. The faster particles move, the hotter things get.

Heat always moves from warmer things to colder things.

Pretend you are holding a warm mug of hot chocolate. The particles in the hot chocolate are moving quickly. They bounce into the particles in the mug. They make them move faster. The mug starts to feel warm. Then, the particles in the mug make the particles in your hand move faster. You feel your hand getting warmer.

1. Heat energy comes from _____.
   a. particles moving faster
   b. particles slowing down

2. Heat energy always moves from something _____ to

   something _____.

3. On each picture, draw arrows showing which way the heat energy is moving.

Name: _____

Light

Have you ever been in a very dark room with no light? What did you see? Nothing! We can't see without light. Light must bounce off objects for us to see them.

Light comes from a **light source**. Anything that makes light energy is a light source. The Sun is a very bright light source. Fire is a light source. Light bulbs are light sources.

Light energy comes out of a light source. It travels in **rays**. Light rays move in a straight line. They only move in one direction.

Imagine you are in a dark room. You are holding a flashlight. When the flashlight is off, you can't see. If you turn the flashlight on, light rays come out. They travel in a straight line. The light rays hit a cat. They bounce back toward you. They go into your eyes. That is how you can see the cat!

1. Light rays always travel in a straight _____.

2. To see things, _____ must bounce off of them and go into our

   _____.

3. Circle the things that are light sources.

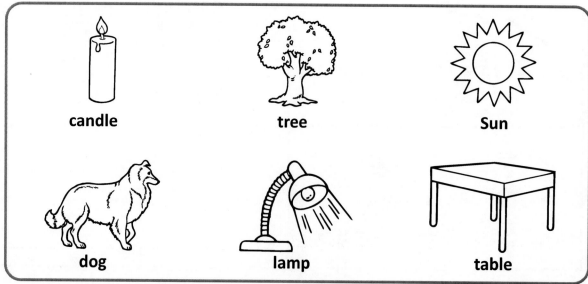

candle	tree	Sun
dog	lamp	table

#8262 Let's Get This Day Started: Science   *©Teacher Created Resources*

Name: _____

Sound

Sounds are made when things vibrate. **Vibrate** means to move back and forth quickly. Sound vibrations travel through the air. They reach our ears, and we hear them.

We usually hear sound that travels through the air. Sound can also travel through liquids and solids. Tap gently on your desk. What does the tapping sound like when it travels through the air to your ear? Put your ear against your desk. Tap gently on the desk again. Does the tapping sound different through the solid?

Sounds can be **loud** or **soft**. A sound is loud when it has a lot of energy. Some loud sounds are a siren and someone yelling. Soft sounds don't have as much energy. Some soft sounds are rain hitting the ground and someone whispering. Rub your hands together. Can you hear the soft sound?

We say that faster vibrations make a **high-pitched** sound. Some high-pitched sounds are birds singing, a baby crying, and a whistle blowing. When things vibrate slower, they make **low-pitched** sounds. Some low-pitched sounds are big drums, a lion's roar, and thunder.

1. *Vibrate* means _____.
    a. to jump up and down fast
    b. to move back and forth quickly
    c. a high-pitched sound

2. Listen to what is going on around you.

    Describe what you *hear*. _____

    Are the sounds *loud* or *soft*? _____

    Are the sounds *high-pitched* or *low-pitched*? _____

Name: _____

What Kind of Energy?

Some things put out light that we can see. Some things create sounds that we can hear. Some things give off heat that we can feel. Most things make more than one kind of energy.

Light and Heat

Most of the time, light and heat go together. The Sun puts out light. We can see the light. It also makes heat. We can feel the heat.

Light and Sound

Some things can put out both light we see and sound we hear. A cell phone puts out light. We can see the screen. It also makes sounds. We can hear it ringing.

Heat and Sound

A few things put out sound we hear and heat we feel. A hairdryer puts out heat. It also puts out sound.

Directions: For each item, circle *light*, *heat*, or *sound*. You may circle more than one kind of energy for some items.

light heat sound	light heat sound	light heat sound
light heat sound	light heat sound	light heat sound
light heat sound	light heat sound	light heat sound

Name: _____

What Do Scientists Do?

Scientists are people who try to answer questions. They want to know how things work. They want to find out why things happen.

What questions do scientists ask? They want to know if plants need the Sun to grow. They wonder what kinds of animals live in a habitat. How does the land on Earth change? How does water move around Earth? Scientists ask all these questions.

How do scientists try to answer their questions? They observe things. This means they use their senses. They look with their eyes and listen with their ears. They record what they observe. They do tests. They use tools to measure how big, fast, or hot things are. Then, they use what they find to try to answer their questions.

When scientists think they have an answer to a question, they share it. They tell other scientists about what they found. They write about it. Science is not a secret! Other scientists can try the same tests to see if they answer the question the same way.

1. Scientists try to answer questions by _____.
   a. observing things   **b.** doing tests   **c.** both **a** and **b**

2. When scientists think they have an answer, they _____

   _____.

3. As a scientist, what questions would you ask?

   _____

   _____

   _____

Name: _____

Data Measurement

When scientists want to answer a question, they do a test. They write down what they observe. The things they write down are called **data**. Scientists look at the data after a test to see if they can answer the question they were testing.

I want to know if mice like to eat cheese or berries. I put some cheese on one side of their cage. I put some berries on the other side. I put some mice in the middle of the cage. I observe the mice for one minute.

1. What data should I record to answer my question? _____

_____

Rupam and Fred want to know if the Sun helps plants grow. They get two plants. They put one by the window where it will get lots of sunlight. They put one in a closet where it will not get any sunlight. They wait one week.

2. What data should they measure to answer their question? _____

_____

3. Circle the tool they should use to measure.

Sarah wants to know if gummy bears will melt in the Sun. She puts five gummy bears in a sunny place. She puts five gummy bears in the shade. She waits one hour.

4. What should Sarah observe and record to answer her question? _____

_____

Donna has a straw, a rubber band, a cotton ball, a piece of paper, and a balloon. She wants to know which materials can stretch.

5. What should Donna do to answer her question? _____

_____

6. What should she record? _____

Name: _____

Interpreting Data

When scientists do a test, they observe what happens. They write it down. The things they write down are called **data**. Scientists look at the data after a test. They try to answer the question they were testing.

Toni and Marcus are making a bridge. They have three materials to choose from. They want to use the longest things to build their bridge. They use a ruler to measure the three things.

Here is their data:

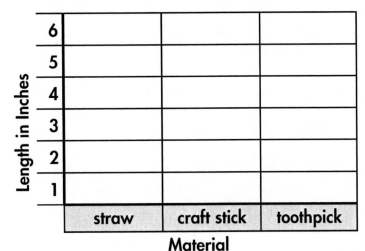

Material		Length of Material
straw		6 inches
craft stick		4 inches
toothpick		2 inches

1. Color in the boxes on the graph using the *data* from the table.

Length in Inches

6			
5			
4			
3			
2			
1			
	straw	craft stick	toothpick

Material

2. Which material is the longest? _____

    How do you know? _____

3. Which material should Toni and Marcus use to build their bridge? _____

    Why? _____

_____

Name: _____

Scientists Look for Patterns

Every day our side of Earth turns toward the Sun. We call that daytime. And every night our side of Earth turns away from the Sun. We call that nighttime. We know that night will always come after day. And day will always come after night. That is a **pattern**. A pattern is something that happens over and over the same way.

Scientists look for patterns to answer questions. Sam wants to know if an ice cube will melt in the sunshine. She puts an ice cube in the sunshine. The ice cube melts. Is this a pattern? Not yet! Sam has only seen this result once. It is not a pattern.

Sam needs to **repeat** the test. This means she must do it again. If she gets the same result three or four times, that is a pattern. She can use this pattern to understand that ice cubes melt in the sunshine.

1. A *pattern* is _____.
    a. something that never happens
    b. something that happens one time
    c. something that happens over and over

2. What season comes next in this pattern?

   spring, summer, fall, winter, spring, summer, _____

3. Why do scientists need to *repeat* tests? _____

   _____

   _____

Name: _____

Cause and Effect

When scientists want to answer a question, they can look for causes and effects.

- A **cause** is a reason why something happened.
- The **effect** is what happened.

Shelby is allergic to cats. She pets a cat. She sneezes.

The *cause* was Shelby petting the cat.

The *effect* was that she sneezed.

Scientists see an effect and want to know what caused it. Why did that plant die? What caused the volcano to erupt? Why did the water evaporate? Here are some causes and effects:

Cause (Why did it happen?)	➡	Effect (What happened?)
A river eroded the rock.	➡	A canyon was formed.
The cactus has sharp spines.	➡	Animals do not eat the cactus.
The winter weather was cold.	➡	The bear slept in its cave.

Directions: Fill in the missing causes and effects. You can use your imagination as long as your answers makes sense.

Cause (Why did it happen?)	➡	Effect (What happened?)
	➡	There was a flood.
He made sure his plant had sunlight and water.	➡	
	➡	The ice cream melted.
There was not enough food in the deer's habitat.	➡	
	➡	We saw a rainbow.

Tracking Sheet

Unit 1 (pages 6–10)		Unit 8 (pages 41–45)		Unit 15 (pages 77–81)	
Traits of Living Things		Insects		What Is a Map?	
What Is a Plant?		Insect Body Parts		Map Keys and Symbols	
What Is an Animal?		Arachnids		Compass Rose	
Plant or Animal?		Crustaceans		What Is a Globe?	
Living or Nonliving?		Gastropods		Comparing Maps and Globes	
Unit 2 (pages 11–15)		**Unit 9 (pages 46–50)**		**Unit 16 (pages 82–86)**	
Parts of Plants		What Are Seasons?		What Are Properties of Materials?	
Parts of Plants We Eat		Summer		Describing Properties of Materials	
Plants Need Sunlight		Fall		Observing with the Senses	
Plants Need Water		Winter		Uses of Materials	
Plants in Different Places		Spring		Changing Properties of Materials	
Unit 3 (pages 16–20)		**Unit 10 (pages 51–55)**		**Unit 17 (pages 87–91)**	
Plant Life Cycles		What Is Weather?		Matter	
Pollination		Weather Reports		Solids	
Seed Dispersal: Wind and Water		Reading a Weather Report		Liquids	
Seed Dispersal: Animals		Dangerous Weather		Gases	
Seed Dispersal: People		Rainbows		Changing States of Matter	
Unit 4 (pages 21–25)		**Unit 11 (pages 56–61)**		**Unit 18 (pages 92–95)**	
Plant Defenses		Slow Changes to Earth: Part 1		Two Kinds of Changes	
Plants That Eat Meat		Slow Changes to Earth: Part 2		Freezing and Melting	
Record-Breaking Plants		Volcanoes		Changes That Can't Be Reversed	
The School Garden		Earthquakes		Can It Change Back?	
Design a Plant		Water Changes the Land		**Unit 19 (pages 96–100)**	
Unit 5 (pages 26–30)		Quick or Slow Change?		Heat, Light, and Sound Energy	
What Animals Need		**Unit 12 (pages 62–66)**		Heat	
Animals Need Oxygen		The Water Cycle		Light	
Animals Need Water		Where Is the Water on Earth?		Sound	
Animals Need Food		Salt Water		What Kind of Energy?	
Animals Need Shelter		Ice on Earth		**Unit 20 (pages 101–105)**	
Unit 6 (pages 31–35)		Keep Water Clean		What Do Scientists Do?	
What Is a Habitat?		**Unit 13 (pages 67–71)**		Data Measurement	
Living and Nonliving Parts of Habitats		Landforms		Interpreting Data	
Omnivores Have Options		Mountains and Hills		Scientists Look for Patterns	
Wet or Dry?		Valleys and Canyons		Cause and Effect	
Migration		Plains			
Unit 7 (pages 36–40)		People Change the Land			
Mammals		**Unit 14 (pages 72–76)**			
Birds		Water on Earth			
Reptiles		Oceans			
Amphibians		Rivers and Streams			
Fish		Lakes			
		People Change Water on Earth			

Answer Key

Unit 1—Living Things

Traits of Living Things (page 6)
1. b
2. themselves
3. Check for appropriate answers.

What Is a Plant? (page 7)
1. c
2. a sunflower plant
3. Yes; Check for appropriate answers.

What Is an Animal? (page 8)
1. a
2. b
3. All animals need food. All animals need air. All animals reproduce.

Plant or Animal? (page 9)

Animals	Plants
Cheetah	Baobab tree
Hummingbird	Raspberry bush
Snail	Barrel cactus
Snake	Dandelion

Living or Nonliving? (page 10)

	Dog	Chair	Rock	Tree
Does it use energy?	Yes	No	No	Yes
Does it need water?	Yes	No	No	Yes
Does it need air?	Yes	No	No	Yes
Does it grow and change?	Yes	No	No	Yes
Does it make more of itself?	Yes	No	No	Yes
Is it living?	Yes	No	No	Yes

Unit 2—All About Plants

Parts of Plants (page 11)
1. a. stem   c. flowers   e. roots
   b. leaves   d. fruit
2. c
3. roots
4. Flowers make seeds that grow new plants.

Parts of Plants We Eat (page 12)
1. root   3. leaf   5. seed
2. flower   4. fruit   6. stem

Plants Need Sunlight (page 13)
1. c
2. water; air
3. They make their own food using sunlight, water, and air.

Plants Need Water (page 14)
1. a
2. water, sunlight, air
3. *Reason 1:* to stay up. *Reason 2:* to make food

Plants in Different Places (page 15)
1. b
2. fires
3. They grow quickly, and they tilt their leaves toward the Sun.

Unit 3—Plant Reproduction

Plant Life Cycles (page 16)
1. c
2. water, air, and warmth
3. shoot, roots, leaves, seeds, new

Pollination (page 17)
1. b
2. egg
3. Pollinators help plants make seeds by moving pollen to an egg in a flower.

Seed Dispersal: Wind and Water (page 18)
1. c
2. They will have a better chance to grow if they move away from their parent plant. They cannot be too crowded by other plants.
3. Check for appropriate answers.

Seed Dispersal: Animals (page 19)
1. c
2. Animals may like to eat the sweet fruit, so they might carry the seeds to new places.
3. The seed sticks to animal fur and falls off somewhere else.

Seed Dispersal: People (page 20)
1. c
2. when people plant seeds and help them grow
3. Check for appropriate answers—students should give evidence, or reasons, for their ideas.

Unit 4—Fun with Plants

Plant Defenses (page 21)
1. b
2. sharp parts, poisons, or working with bugs
3. Thorns protect or defend them from being eaten by some animals.

Plants That Eat Meat (page 22)
1. a
2. It can trap the bug between leaves or catch bugs in sticky liquid.
3. They live where the soil doesn't have enough nutrients, so they get nutrients from digesting bugs and small animals.

Record-Breaking Plants (page 23)
1. c
2. 70 inches
3. Check for appropriate answers.

The School Garden (page 24)
1. a
2. Plants need sunlight to grow.
3. They watered the plants and pulled out the weeds.

Answer Key *(cont.)*

Design a Plant (page 25)
Make certain students have checked off and included each plant part.

Unit 5—Animal Needs

What Animals Need (page 26)
1. a
2. oxygen, water, food, shelter
3. Check for appropriate answers.

Animals Need Oxygen (page 27)
1. b
2. water
3. Oxygen helps turn food into energy.

Animals Need Water (page 28)
1. b
2. by drinking; in the food they eat
3. Check for appropriate answers.

Animals Need Food (page 29)
Check arrows. All arrows should be pointing to the right.

Animals Need Shelter (page 30)
1. c
2. to keep them safe from weather; to keep them safe from predators
3. Check for appropriate answers.

Unit 6—Animal Habitats

What Is a Habitat? (page 31)
1. a
2. food, shelter
3. Check for appropriate answers.

Living and Nonliving Parts of Habitats (page 32)
Check lists for appropriate answers. The following should be included:
1. *Living:* trees, whale
   Nonliving: air, mountains, rocks, snow
2. *Living:* camels, plants, trees
   Nonliving: air, dirt, rocks, sand

Omnivores Have Options (page 33)
1. b
2. survival
3. They eat many kinds of food. If one kind of food runs out, they can eat other kinds.

Wet or Dry? (page 34)
1. c
2. food
3. Check for appropriate answers.

Migration (page 35)
1. c
2. whale; zebra; Arctic tern
   Check for appropriate regional answers such as geese or butterflies.
3. warm; food

Unit 7—Vertebrate Animals

Mammals (page 36)
1. b
2. milk
3. I am warm-blooded, have hair, and drank milk when I was a baby.

Birds (page 37)
1. c
2. swim
3. Feathers keep a bird warm or cool, keep water off, and help some birds fly.

Reptiles (page 38)
1. c
2. adult
3. Reptile skin does not grow and stretch. They shed their old skins when they are too small. They have new, bigger skins underneath.

Amphibians (page 39)
1. b
2. lungs; skin
3. Amphibians catch small prey with their sticky tongues and swallow them whole.

Fish (page 40)
1. c
2. fresh
3. Fish have gills and cannot breathe air.

Unit 8—Invertebrate Animals

Insects (page 41)
1. c
2. insects
3. Insects have four wings that are part of their exoskeleton. Birds have two wings with feathers.

Insect Body Parts (page 42)

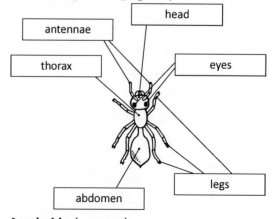

Arachnids (page 43)
1. c
2. eight; two
3. Insects have six legs and three body parts. Arachnids have eight legs and two body parts. Insects can have wings and antennae, but arachnids do not.

Answer Key *(cont.)*

Crustaceans (page 44)
1. a
2. exoskeleton
3. Check for appropriate answers.

Gastropods (page 45)
1. b
2. poisonous
3. Gastropods scrape the radula on their food, and it rips the food into tiny pieces.

Unit 9—Seasons
What Are Seasons? (page 46)

summer   fall   winter   spring

Summer (page 47)
1. c
2. longest
3. Check for appropriate answers.

Fall (page 48)
1. b
2. shorter; cooler
3. Check for appropriate answers.

Winter (page 49)
1. a
2. sleep
3. Check for appropriate answers.

Spring (page 50)
1. b
2. longer; sunshine
3. Check for appropriate answers.

Unit 10—Weather
What Is Weather? (page 51)
1. b
2. tiny droplets of water
3. Check for appropriate answers.

Weather Reports (page 52)
1. c
2. Check for appropriate answers.
3. Check for appropriate answers.

Reading a Weather Report (page 53)
1. 75 degrees and partly cloudy
2. Thursday
3. Tuesday

Dangerous Weather (page 54)
1. b
2. storms, hurricanes, blizzards, floods (any 3)
3. Check for appropriate answers.

Rainbows (page 55)
1. water drops and sunlight
2. You can't touch a rainbow because it is made of light.
3. The rainbow should be colored in the correct color order.

Unit 11—Earth Changes
Slow Changes to Earth: Part 1 (page 56)
No questions.

Slow Changes to Earth: Part 2 (page 57)
Weathering: breaks it; weathering is when rocks break into smaller pieces.
Erosion: takes it; erosion is when the small bits of rock are moved from one place to another.
Deposition: drops it; deposition is when the small bits of rock are dropped in a new place.

Volcanoes (page 58)
1. c
2. quickly
3. They can make new rocks, bury land, and make new islands.

Earthquakes (page 59)
1. a
2. crust; rock
3. An earthquake can make cracks in the ground, make a stream change course, and break roads. It can also knock down buildings.

Water Changes the Land (page 60)
1. Waves can wear away rocks near the ocean; glaciers can move rocks; rivers can carve canyons. (any 2)
2. Rainstorms can wash away dirt; floods can wash away dirt and change the way rivers flow; tsunamis can pull rocks and dirt into the ocean.
3. A glacier moves very slowly. It is made of ice. A tsunami is a wave of water that moves very quickly.

Quick or Slow Change? (page 61)

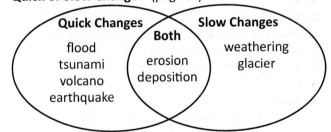

Note: If students have different answers, ask them to explain their answers. Accept if plausible.

Answer Key (cont.)

Unit 12—Water on Earth
The Water Cycle (page 62)

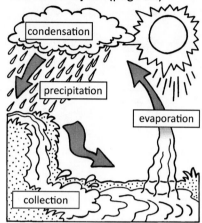

Where Is the Water on Earth? (page 63)
1. a
2. We can't use most of the water on Earth because it is salt water.
3. Check for appropriate answers.

Salt Water (page 64)
1. b
2. salt; oceans
3. Oceans are important because many animals live there.

Ice on Earth (page 65)
1. sea ice   2. iceberg   3. glacier

Keep Water Clean (page 66)
1. c
2. Our water can come from under the ground or from lakes and rivers. Accept other answers appropriate for your area.
3. Check for appropriate answers.

Unit 13—Landforms
Landforms (page 67)
1. c
2. same; changing
3. Wind and water break rocks into smaller pieces. The small pieces get moved to new places.

Mountains and Hills (page 68)
1. a
2. range
3. Mountains can be made when edges of the plates of Earth's crust push up; Volcanoes can make mountains.

Valleys and Canyons (page 69)
1. c
2. canyon
3. Glaciers drag rocks that grind away some of the land.

Plains (page 70)
1. c
2. rivers
3. Wind and rain break down the lava rock into soil so grass can grow.

People Change the Land (page 71)
1. People cut down trees to clear land for farming, for building, and for making paper. (any 2)
2. People change the land to grow food, get wood, build roads, and get oil and minerals. (any 2)
3. erosion

Unit 14—Bodies of Water
Water on Earth (page 72)
1. b
2. streams; lakes
3. Because it is mostly covered with water, which looks blue.

Oceans (page 73)
1. c
2. surface
3. Rain water carries salt from rocks down rivers into the ocean.

Rivers and Streams (page 74)
1. a
2. downhill
3. Rivers can wear away dirt and rock to make canyons. They can drop lots of dirt and rock.

Lakes (page 75)
1. a
2. dam
3. The water does not flow out. It evaporates and leaves a lot of salt behind.

People Change Water on Earth (page 76)
1. c
2. dam
3. We need water to live. We drink, cook, and clean with water. We use it to grow food.

Unit 15—Maps
What Is a Map? (page 77)
1. Check the coloring on the map for land (green or brown) and for water (blue).
2. Wilderness Park
3. on the map key
4. mountain
5. compass rose

Answer Key *(cont.)*

Map Keys and Symbols (page 78)
1. plains
2. river; check for correct symbol
3. one; check for correct symbol
4. Check for mountains east of the canyon.
5. Check that students have added a symbol for "town" to the key.
6. Check that students have added a town to the map.

Compass Rose (page 79)
1.

2. east
3. south
4. East
5. Check that student directions work.

What Is a Globe? (page 80)
Check the globe for appropriate colors and arrows.

Comparing Maps and Globes (page 81)

Map
- flat
- may only show small areas
- shows more details
- has a map key
- easy to carry

Both
- helps us find places
- gives us information about a place

Globe
- round
- shows the whole planet
- shows fewer details
- hard to carry

Unit 16—Properties of Materials

What Are Properties of Materials? (page 82)
Possible labels and sorting:
Round: marble, ball, orange
Square: sandwich, box, cracker

Describing Properties of Materials (page 83)
Students will share answers with partners. Assist if needed.

Observing with the Senses (page 84)
Check for appropriate answers.

Uses of Materials (page 85)
1. Check that students have listed some soft materials.
2. Check that students have chosen appropriate materials.
3. Check for appropriate reasons.
4. Check bridge drawings for accuracy.

Changing Properties of Materials (page 86)
1. *Possible answers:* squish, pull, tear, roll, pinch
2. *Possible answers:* fold, cut, tear, crumple, ball, wrinkle
3. *Possible answers:* tie, knot, bend, pull, cut

Unit 17—States of Matter

Matter (page 87)
1. particles
2. solid, liquid, gas
3. wood–solid
   orange juice–liquid
   steam–gas
   river–liquid
   shoe–solid
   oxygen–gas

Solids (page 88)
1. particles
2. sugar, sand
3. Three solids in my body are bones, teeth, and hair.

Liquids (page 89)
1. a
2. Check for appropriate answers.
3. A liquid can flow and pour because its particles stay close together, but not in the same position. They can slip and slide around.

Gases (page 90)
1. c
2. air, steam, oxygen
3. You burp when extra air in your lungs and stomach comes out.

Changing States of Matter (page 91)
1. a solid   2. a liquid   3. a gas
4. The particles stop moving and stick together.

Unit 18—Reversible and Irreversible Changes

Two Kinds of Changes (page 92)
1. a
2. b
3. Yes, it can be reversed. You can let the air out of the balloon, and the balloon will go back to the way it was before.

Freezing and Melting (page 93)
1. c   2. b   3. b   4. a

Changes That Can't Be Reversed (page 94)
1. c
2. Check for appropriate answers.
3. Check for appropriate answers.

Can It Change Back? (page 95)
1. No, the eggs cannot change back to being raw.
2. Yes, she can make the chocolate solid if she puts it in the refrigerator.
3. No, Mateo can never grow younger.
4. Yes, Althea can make the ice pop into juice by leaving it out for a while. It will melt.
5. Yes, the water vapor in the clouds will become rain.

Answer Key *(cont.)*

Unit 19—Heat, Light, and Sound Energy
Heat, Light, and Sound Energy (page 96)
1. *Possible answers:* Energy makes things move and change, cooks your food, makes the Sun shine, makes you move and grow. (any 2)
2. see
3. hear
4. feel
5. Check for appropriate drawings.
6. Check for appropriate drawings.
7. Check for appropriate drawings.

Heat (page 97)
1. a
2. warmer, colder
3.

Light (page 98)
1. line
2. light rays; eyes
3. lamp, candle, Sun

Sound (page 99)
1. b
2. Check for appropriate answers.

What Kind of Energy? (page 100)
flute – sound
fire – all 3
iron – heat (sound may also come from steam)
toaster – heat (maybe light: the coils glow red)
firecracker – all 3
TV – light and sound
flashlight – light
popcorn – heat and sound
kettle – heat and sound

Unit 20—About Science
What Do Scientists Do? (page 101)
1. c
2. share it and write about it
3. Check for appropriate answers.

Data Measurement (page 102)
1. They should list how many mice went to eat the cheese and how many mice went to eat the berries.
2. They should measure how tall the plants are at the end of the test.
3. ruler
4. She should record what the gummy bears look like and if they melted.
5. She should try to stretch each material.
6. She should record which materials can stretch and which can't.

Interpreting Data (page 103)
1.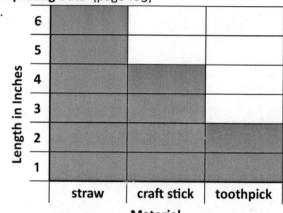
2. The straw because it is 6 inches. It has more bars filled on the graph.
3. Accept any answer as long as the student gives a valid reason.

Scientists Look for Patterns (page 104)
1. c
2. fall
3. Scientists repeat tests so they can see a pattern in their results.

Cause and Effect (page 105)
Answers will vary but may include:

Cause (Why did it happen?) ➡ **Effect** (What happened?)

Cause		Effect
It rained a lot.	➡	There was a flood.
He made sure his plant had sunlight and water.	➡	**His plant grew tall.**
The ice cream was left out in the sunshine.	➡	The ice cream melted.
There was not enough food in the deer's habitat.	➡	**The deer was hungry.**
It stopped raining and the Sun came out.	➡	We saw a rainbow.